The Ultimate
BQC
Book of Knowledge

Derek O'Brien was born in Kolkata. He began his professional career as a journalist for *Sportsworld* magazine but soon shifted to advertising. After working for a number of very successful years as Creative Head of Ogilvy, Derek decided to focus all his energy and talent in his passion—quizzing.

Today, Derek O'Brien is Asia's best-known quizmaster and the CEO of Derek O'Brien & Associates. He is the host of the longest-running game show on Indian television, the Bournvita Quiz Contest, for which he was voted the Best Anchor of a Game Show at the Indian Television Academy Awards for three years in a row. He also hosts the longest-running corporate quiz show, the Economic Times Brand Equity Quiz. Always innovating and keeping abreast with the times, Derek is also credited with having conducted the first quiz on Twitter in 2010.

Derek O'Brien has written several best-selling reference and quiz books. He is also the author of two extremely successful school textbook series, *Know and Grow with Derek* and *Be a GK Champ*.

In 2011, Derek O'Brien was voted to the Rajya Sabha as a Member of Parliament (MP).

THE ULTIMATE

BOOK OF KNOWLEDGE

DEREK O'BRIEN

RUPA

First published in 2012 by
Rupa Publications India Pvt. Ltd.
7/16, Ansari Road, Daryaganj
New Delhi 110002

Sales Centres:

Allahabad Bengaluru Chennai
Hyderabad Jaipur Kathmandu
Kolkata Mumbai

ISBN 978-81-291-2039-7

10 9 8 7 6 5 4 3 2 1

CONTENTS

FOREWORD

As we celebrate forty incredible years of the Bournvita Quiz Contest this year, it gives me immense pleasure in introducing to you *The Ultimate Bournvita Quiz Contest Book of Knowledge*.

Since its launch in 1948, Cadbury Bournvita has been one of India's most loved and trusted brands. For over six decades, the brand has been an enduring symbol of mental and physical health and all-round development. In 1972, Cadbury India introduced the Bournvita Quiz Contest (BQC) as a radio programme. Following its tremendous success on radio, the programme found a new avatar on television in 1994. After a hiatus of a few years and following the compelling public movement to 'Bring back BQC', 2011 saw the return of India's favourite quiz contest to national television.

During the last forty years, this show has touched the lives of over 12 lakh children and millions of loyal viewers through its 600+ television episodes. A number of reputed personalities and celebrities from the fields of cinema, music, sports and politics have also made special appearances on the show.

The Ultimate Bournvita Quiz Contest Book of

Knowledge comes to you in two volumes, with a compilation of questions asked on BQC from 1994 to 2010. So if you think you have an unquenchable thirst for knowledge, an openness to learn anything new and a knack for facts, I am sure you will enjoy this book!

I would like to take this opportunity to thank the team from Derek O'Brien & Associates for producing this book. I would also like to thank the millions of viewers, students, principals and teachers for their love and support, which in turn has made the Bournvita Quiz Contest a household name!

Happy quizzing!

Anand Kripalu
President, India & South East Asia
Cadbury India Limited

INTRODUCTION

The Bournvita Quiz Contest (BQC) made its debut as a radio programme in 1972. From radio it moved to television in 1994, and has been a part of our lives for nearly forty years now. Over the years, as the show won multiple awards for Best Children's programme and Best Host, my team and I have lived and grown with it. To celebrate these decades of making knowledge fun, we bring you an exhaustive compilation of questions in two volumes. In *The Ultimate Bournvita Quiz Contest Book of Knowledge* Volumes 1 and 2, we have brought together over 3,000 questions asked on television, from the very first show in 1994 right until 2010.

It has been great fun, yet hard work, putting together these two volumes. My colleagues and I have burnt the proverbial midnight oil, while enjoying the nostalgia of sifting through stacks of old questions and looking through hours of tapes. So much has changed over the years, since 1994: the participants, the sets, the format, even the way I look...I have the very able and stunning Saumya Tandon as co-quizmaster now, and we have gone bilingual. But the very core of the Bournvita Quiz Contest, which is a quiz with a simple, uncomplicated and classic format, has remained untouched. And that is what makes BQC special!

The questions included in these two volumes are ones we felt would always entertain and educate students and quiz lovers. I have loved asking each one of these questions, and hope you will enjoy reading them too.

Thank you!

With every good wish,

Derek O'Brien

P.S. Stay in touch with me through www.twitter.com, my handle is @quizderek.

HALL OF FAME

PAST WINNERS OF THE BOURNVITA
QUIZ CONTEST

1994–1995, Mumbai
Campion High School, Mumbai
Balakrishnan Sivaraman, Sudhanshu Bhuwalka

1995–1996, Mumbai
Kendriya Vidyalaya, Powai, Mumbai
Eipy Koshy, Gourav Shah

1996–1997, Mumbai
Bombay International High School, Mumbai
Nirica Borges, Advait Behara

1997, Mumbai
Mount Saint Mary's School, New Delhi
Joe Christy, Maninder Singh Jessel

1997–1998, Mumbai
Bombay Scottish High School, Mumbai
Shaambhavi Pandyaa, Rahul Lalmalani

1998, Mumbai
Sacred Heart Convent School, Jamshedpur
Ela Verma, Lavanya Raghavan

1998–1999, Mumbai
Indian School Al Ghubra, Muscat
Anand Raghavan, Hitesh Kanvatirtha

1999, Mumbai
Maneckji Cooper High School, Mumbai
Ipsita Bandopadhyay, Gourav Bhattacharya

1999–2000, Mumbai
Chettinad Vidyashram, Chennai
Siddharth, Karthik Das

2000–2001, Mumbai
Bharatiya Vidya Bhavan, Hyderabad
Ananya Bhaskar, Aksha Anand

2001 September, Mumbai
Brightlands, Dehradun
Ankur Bharadwaj, Shray Sharma

2001 December, Mumbai
Little Flower High School, Hyderabad
G. Mithilesh, K. Siddharth Reddy

2002 February, Bentota, Sri Lanka
G.D. Birla Centre For Education, Kolkata
Namrata Basu, Rituparna Dey

2002 June, Mumbai
Kerala Samajam Public School, Jamshedpur
Saurav Biswas, Kunal Mohan

2002 September, Mumbai
Jamnabai Narsee School, Mumbai
Sharan Narayanan, Vishnu Shrest

2003 January, Kerala
Naval Public High School, Mumbai
Apoorva Sharma, Abhishek Pandit

2003 May, Kolkata
St Patrick's Higher Secondary School, Asansol
Pushpen Dasgupta, Shamik Ray

2003 October, Sangla
St Agnes Loreto Day School, Lucknow
Aastha Srivastava, Illa Gupta

2004 February, Swabhumi, Kolkata
Apeejay School, Jalandhar
Mohit Thukral, Sahil Sareen

2004 May, Goa
Springdales School, Delhi
Anirudh Sridhar, B. Anuraag

2004 July, Indian Military Academy, Dehradun
The Mother's International School, Delhi
Krittika Adhikary, Milind Ganjoo

2004 November, Kolkata
Amity International School, New Delhi
Aishwarya Singhal, Adarsh Modi

2005 February, Kolkata
St Kabir, Ahmedabad
Yogarshi Vyas, Helish Sharma

2005 May, Kolkata
Brightlands, Dehradun
Akshay Sharma, Avantika Singh

2005 August, Kolkata
Amity International, New Delhi
Utkarsh Johari, Aishwarya Singhal

2006 July, Kolkata
Riverdale High School, Dehradun
Kartikeya Panwar, Sumit Nair

2006 November, Kolkata
Seth Jaipuria School, Lucknow
Ratnaksha Lele, Ananya Kumar Singh

2011 August, Kolkata
Amity International School, Noida
Kripi Badonia, Shinjini Biswas

2012 January, Kolkata
Birla Vidya Niketan, New Delhi
Anusha Malhotra, Nitya Bansal

CREDITS

DIRECTOR	Derek O'Brien
CO-QUIZMASTER	Saumya Tandon
CREATIVE DIRECTOR	Shrradha Kulkarni
EXECUTIVE PRODUCERS	Andrew Scolt
	Nayan Chaudhury
	Sunil Shah
PRODUCER	Prabuddha Chatterjee (Gulu)
ONLINE DIRECTOR	Dongrej Gor
DOP	R. Diwakaran
SOUND	Ashwyn Balsaver
	Seby Fernandes
SENIOR ASSOCIATES, RESEARCH	Amit Ghosh
	Shalini Chaudhury
ASSOCIATES, RESEARCH	Anik Ghosal
	Srirupa Roy
	Ayashman Dey
	Nilanjana Basu
	Ammar Hamid
	Natasha Gasper
SENIOR RELATIONSHIP ASSOCIATES	Shane Alliew
	Heena Ade (Israni)

RELATIONSHIP ASSOCIATES	Fatema Marfatia
	Calvin Tully
	Laressa Gomez
	Sean Augustine
	Durjoy Guha
	Dipankar Rao
	Conrad Pote
	Sheldon Alliew
	Ishita Bose Chakraborty
	Aubrey Whyte
	Daniel Johns
	Fionna Sayers
	Michael Blacquiere
	Tapan Roy
SENIOR ASSOCIATE, FINANCE	Kalyanmoy Hazra
PRODUCTION ASSOCIATES	Sreevalsa Menon
	Shane Baptiste
	Vinu Joseph
	Supriyo Nandi
	Victor Bhat
SENIOR ASSOCIATE, DESIGN	Mahua Basu
SAUMYA'S HAIR & MAKE-UP ARTIST	Elton Fernandez
SAUMYA'S WARDROBE	Kiran Uttam Ghosh
OPERATIVE	B. Lokabiraman
CAMERAMEN	Bhagyawan
	Anandan
	D. Nandakumar
	Debabrata Paul
	Sridhar

HINDI SCRIPT	Rajneesh Kaushal
OFFLINE EDITORS	Vivek Iyer
	Bhavin Patel
JIMMY JIB	Arshad Shaikh
	Saleem Syed
MUSIC	Shankar, Ehsaan, Loy
ASST TO DOP	Selvaraj Xavier
	J. Selvam
SET DESIGN & FABRICATION	Kosmos India
HD EQUIPMENT	Kaliedoxcope
SOUND, LIGHTS & AV	Friends Of Shiva
SHOT AT	Aurora Studio
PRODUCTION ASSISTANTS	Pabitra
	Mrinal
	Saha
	Jha
	Sudip
MAKE-UP	Babu

INDIA

1. Which famous mausoleum was called 'a teardrop on the cheek of time' by Rabindranath Tagore?
2. Name the Chinese pilgrim who came to India during the reign of Chandragupta II.
3. In the Lok Sabha, whom do members address their speeches to?
4. By what name is the Baha'i Temple in New Delhi popularly known?
5. The 1998 nuclear tests were conducted by India at Pokhran. What was the site of the 1974 set of tests?
6. In India, what is the name of the document that lists all the cases and punishments that a person committing any crime is liable to be charged with?
7. M. Karunanidhi was the chief minister of which state in India?
8. If the Republic Day parade starts from Raisina Hill near the Rashtrapati Bhawan, where does it end?
9. Which Nobel laureate passed away in Kolkata on 5 September 1997?
10. Which Indian festival is known as Shigmo in Goa, Madan Daman or Kamayan in south India, and Dol Jatra in West Bengal?

11. Name the mausoleum of Muhammad Adil Shah which distinctly echoes even the faintest whisper over ten times.
12. What is the difference between a 'chowk' and a 'chowkidar'?
13. Which national park was established as Hailey National Park in 1936?
14. What is the difference between a 'hookah' and a 'howdah'?
15. Who was appointed as the Dewan of Baroda in 1874?
16. Pushkar is famous for its camel fair. What is Etawah famous for?
17. Which district in India, bound by Mandi and Kullu in the north, Kinnaur in the east, and the state of Uttarakhand in the south, derives its name from a town?
18. What is the difference between 'gopi' and 'gopuram'?
19. Shakti Sthal is the samadhi of which prime minister of India?
20. The Golden Chariot train is named after the famous Stone Chariot in Hampi. In which state is Hampi located?
21. In which Indian state would you find the Bandhavgarh National Park?
22. Whose birth anniversary is celebrated as International Nurses Day?
23. Which city, located in Jharkhand, is considered to be India's first planned industrial city?
24. Which Mughal emperor was nominated as the governor of the Deccan in 1617?
25. Which state came into existence on 15 November 2000 as the twenty-eighth state of the Indian Union?

26. The rest of southeast Asia calls it a 'trishaw'. What do we call it in India?

27. In India, 'Duty Unto Death' is the motto of which organization?

28. The name of which mountain peak in Tamil Nadu means 'big mountain' in the Badugu language?

29. The name of which script used in northwestern India literally means 'from the mouth of the Guru'?

30. In terms of the currency notes of India, if MG Series is Mahatma Gandhi Series, what is AP Series?

31. In which present-day state of India did calico, a type of cotton cloth, originate?

32. Who was the first deputy prime minister of India?

33. In which Indian state would you be if you saw the Vithala Temple with musical pillars, a monolithic chariot, and a stone platform called the Mahanavami Dibba?

34. The name of which disease is derived from the Greek words meaning 'half head'?

35. Which Indian world champion now lives in Spain and is nicknamed 'Vishy, the Tiger from Madras'?

36. If you visited Arjuna's Penance, which temple town would you be in?

37. Which king wrote *Amuktamalyada*?

38. Which Indian prime minister was born near Varanasi but died in the capital of Uzbekistan?

39. 'Chippiparai' is a breed of which animal found in south India?

40. Which city in northeastern India was once known as Pragyotishpura (the eastern city of light)?

41. In which state is the famous Ramoji Rao Film City located?

4 • THE ULTIMATE BQC BOOK OF KNOWLEDGE

42. Which Indian cricketer won the Arjuna Award in 1975, the Padma Bhushan in 1980, and became Wisden Cricketer of the Year in 1980?
43. Which branch of the Ministry of Defence was set up as an Armed Force of the Union in 1978 on recommendations of the Rustamji Committee?
44. How are the outer Himalayas better known?
45. What was the name of the silent non-violent protest against the destruction of forests of Uttar Pradesh in 1973?
46. What is the difference between a 'haveli' and a 'havildar'?
47. In the 1984 parliamentary elections, which famous person did Madhavrao Scindia defeat in the Gwalior constituency?
48. Who is the famous father of Zakir Hussain, the musician?
49. In Hindu mythology, Shakuntala was the daughter of which apsara?
50. What is the state bird of Arunachal Pradesh?

Answers on pages 134–136

SPORTS

1. Which English soccer club won the English Premier League for the most number of times between 1992 and 2012?

2. In 2001, whose record did Mohammed Ashraful of Bangladesh break, to become the youngest cricketer to score a Test century on his debut match (he was seventeen years and sixty-one days)?

3. Harsh Mankad represented India in the Davis Cup. In which sport did his father, Ashok Mankad, represent India?

4. Whom did Han Jian lose to at the 1981 badminton World Cup final at Kuala Lumpur?

5. In 1998, whose record did Paramjit Singh break, to become the national record holder in the 400 metre race?

6. Who is the first Indian driver to test-drive for a Formula One team?

7. Bora Milutinovic has coached four different countries in the World Cup soccer finals. Which was the fifth country he coached, that qualified for the 2002 World Cup?

8. Complete the list: Don Budge, Fred Perry, Roy Emerson, Rod Laver, Andre Agassi, Roger Federer and...

9. Spiridon Louis won the marathon gold in the first modern Olympics at Athens in 1896. Which country did he represent?

10. Whom did Zimbabwe defeat in the first-ever Cricket World Cup match they played in 1983?

11. Who was the next Ferrari driver to win the Formula 1 championship after Jody Scheckter won it in 1979?

12. Jan-Ove Waldner was a double world champion in which indoor sport?

13. In 2001, who became the first Indian girl to be the world junior chess champion?

14. Who holds the record for winning the most number of men's singles titles in the National Table Tennis Championship?

15. In 1982–83, which Indian batsman scored 1,182 runs in 11 away Test matches?

16. Who were the first Indian women chess players to qualify for the men's National 'A' Championship Tournament in 2001?

17. Who was the first male athlete to win the 400 metre gold in successive Olympics?

18. In which sport were Misha Grewal and Bhuvaneshwari Kumari women's national champions?

19. In the Asian Games, India has won the gold medal in hockey twice. In which city did they win?

20. Which is the first city to have hosted the Winter Olympic Games twice?

21. In which card game can you score a Grand Slam?

22. Which Indian had the honour of bowling the first ball in the history of the Cricket World Cup?

23. The Camp Nou stadium is home to which European soccer club?
24. Who was the first Indian to win the World Amateur Snooker Championship in 1984?
25. Stefan Edberg is a former Swedish tennis player. But Stefan Effenberg was a famous_____
26. Who is the youngest person to captain India in a Test match?
27. Who led India to victory in the one Test match he captained in 1987–88?
28. Who was the first person to win the Arjuna Award for badminton?
29. Which famous basketball player led the Los Angeles Lakers to five championships in the 1980s?
30. In 1992, who became the first sponsored neutral umpire in Test cricket?
31. Syd, Millie and Olly were the mascots of the Olympic Games in 2000. If Millie is short for Millennium, what do the other two words signify?
32. In the UK, if Wimbledon is the best-known tennis tournament, which is the most prestigious badminton tournament in the UK since 1899?
33. Azharuddin was the second cricketer to score 8,000 runs in One Day Internationals. Who was the first?
34. After which professional cricketer is the stadium at St John's Wood in London named?
35. Describe how a linesman would indicate an offside in football.
36. Who was the first cricketer to score a century in a Cricket World Cup match?
37. At the 1998 FIFA World Cup final match, who scored

the third goal for France after Zinedine Zidane had scored the first two?

38. In which game does 'powerplay' mean a temporary situation in which a team has a numerical advantage over its opponents because one or more players is serving a penalty?

39. Why did some countries boycott the 1980 Moscow Olympics?

40. Who was the first black man to win the singles title at Wimbledon, the US Open and Australian Open?

41. To what does the following routine apply: talk-throw-reach-wade-row-swim-tow-carry?

42. In which sport would you come across AFF or Accelerated Freefall Course?

43. In which Olympic sport does the competitor aim for a target placed at a distance of 70 metres?

44. How would you run out a batsman when he takes a run even after both bails are off?

45. What is boardsailing also known as?

46. Who missed a perfect 100 Test average by just four runs?

47. Which country's football team is nicknamed the 'Socceroos'?

48. In which event did Mohini Bhardwaj, representing the USA, win a silver medal at the 2004 Athens Olympics?

49. What is the longest running event entirely on a track at the Olympic Games?

50. In 1998, who was awarded the Arjuna Award for football?

Answers on pages 136–137

WHAT'S THE QUESTION 1

1. Name literally means 'person of the forest'
2. Another name for asteroids
3. This chief minister's father was the chief minister of Jammu and Kashmir between 1996 and 2002.
4. Starchy substance obtained by heating cassava roots
5. US portrait painter known for his dot-and-dash code system
6. First Indian to play professional football in England
7. A doughnut-shaped fried snack from southern India
8. *Jungle Book*'s 'great grey lone wolf'
9. In India, it is also known as the 'Car Festival'.
10. It appeared on the Chinese flag till 1911.
11. Griffin's Wharf, Boston, 1773
12. It is the Russian word for 'fortress'.
13. He built a part of his own mausoleum (tomb) at Sikandra.
14. The Japanese word for 'tray planting'.
15. Domesticated ox-like mammal with shaggy hair sometimes called grunting ox
16. Possibly the world's most popular sausage, also called wiener (Hint: German city)
17. The most important carbohydrate in the body

18. The hero of Toyland
19. Yamunanagar is a district of this Indian state.
20. Dromedary and Bactrian
21. Literally means 'great soul' in Hindi
22. It is the highest continuously active volcano in the world.
23. 'Hum Sab Bharatiye Hain, Hum Sab Bharatiye Hain' is the song of this institution.
24. Acronym for 'Write Once Read Many'
25. The land of the Maori tribe
26. This event was also called the Amritsar Massacre.
27. Pituitary, thyroid and adrenal are some of these glands.
28. In Hindu mythology, he gave Saraswati her name.
29. Akbar's revenue minister who was also well known as Sher Shah's military engineer.
30. Sinhalese and Tamil are this country's two national languages.
31. According to the National Emblem of India, this animal is the guardian of the east.
32. This mathematical term means 'parts in each hundred'.
33. The name of this civilization in Greek means 'between rivers'.
34. This dance form of India was earlier known as sadir dasi attam.
35. Official office of the president of the United States
36. Second tallest land animal
37. Petruchio and Katherina (Hint: Literature)
38. This famous dog was created by Charles Monroe Schulz.

39. He has nephews named Morty and Ferdy.
40. The word comes from 'Radio Detection and Ranging'.
41. This elephant is the mascot of the Indian Railways.
42. 'Citius, Altius, Fortius' is the motto of these games.
43. He shifted his capital to Daulatabad in 1327.
44. 'An adventure 65 million years in the making' (Hint: Film)
45. This Belgian detective made his last appearance in the book *Curtain.*
46. The International Society for Krishna Consciousness
47. The first to enter all four pieces in the home square wins.
48. He murdered his brother Bleda in 445 CE to become a Hun ruler.
49. Stalinabad was the former capital of this country.
50. A widely used email service co-founded by Sabeer Bhatia in 1996.

Answers on pages 137–139

SCIENCE

1. Over 70 per cent of the population of greater one-horned rhinos occurs in which national park?
2. What are the spots on a leopard commonly called?
3. What did Van Helmont describe as 'something which cannot be confined in a vessel nor reduced to a visible body'?
4. The functioning of hydraulic brakes is based on which principle?
5. Which gland swells to a goitre?
6. Which scientist was offered the presidency of Israel after Chaim Weizmann's death in 1952?
7. A species of which plant is known as prickly pear?
8. Why didn't Alexander Graham Bell's mother or his wife use the telephone he invented?
9. The hammer, anvil and stirrup are bones in which organ of the human body?
10. In 1907, which scientist joined the Indian finance department as assistant accountant general?
11. Using a bowl of water, how can you tell a good egg from a bad one?
12. Barnacle Bill, Yogi, Casper and Scooby-Doo were

some of the names given to the rock samples on which celestial body?

13. How did Armalcolite, a mineral from the moon, get its name?
14. Who invented the process of pasteurization?
15. The Latin name for which metal is cuprum?
16. In Einstein's equation $E=mc^2$, what does 'c' stand for?
17. Helium, neon, argon, krypton and xenon belong to which set of gases?
18. What is the household term for acetic acid?
19. Which animal gets its name from the Afrikaans words for 'jump' and 'goat'?
20. Which two gases react to give water?
21. Cerebellum and cerebrum are parts of which organ in the human body?
22. What might you see when refraction occurs during precipitation?
23. Whose first patented invention was the Electrical Vote Recorder?
24. In physics, what would the mass of an object multiplied by its velocity give you?
25. Which is the largest joint in the human body?
26. After which scientist did NASA name the third of its four 'Great Observatories'?
27. The first thing you would have to do is sit down and lean forward if you suddenly experienced what is medically called epistaxis. What would have happened?
28. Pupil, iris and cornea are parts of which organ in the human body?
29. Which breed of dog is also called the Congo Bush dog?

30. What, in a doctor's prescription, is often expressed as 120/80?
31. On a computer keyboard, if 'ctrl' is control, what is 'alt'?
32. In which film does Shah Rukh Khan play a scientist from NASA?
33. Which vegetable is also called aubergine?
34. With which numeral does @ share a key on a standard keyboard?
35. Which animal's arms are joined at their base by a web of tissue known as the skirt?
36. If the salt you are eating is lacking in 'I', what is it lacking in?
37. Scurvy is caused due to a deficiency of which vitamin in the human body?
38. Which is the longest bone in the human body?
39. What does the human liver secrete about 800 to 1,000 millilitres of?
40. Which is the most widely used of all solvents?
41. Which famous scientist, born in 1893, was a member of the first Lok Sabha from West Bengal?
42. In computers, what does 'cc' in an email stand for?
43. About 99 per cent of which element in the human body is held in the bones and teeth?
44. The Latin word 'vacca' meaning cow, gives us which term in medicine?
45. In the human body, what is expressed by the formula 2123-2123?
46. If the domain name is 'au', which country does it have its origin in?
47. Which is the first element in the periodic table?

48. If healthy, which organ of the human body will float in water?

49. The satellites of Uranus are named after characters from the works of Alexander Pope or_____

50. How many atoms are there in one molecule of water?

Answers on pages 139–141

FUN FACTS 1

1. The bee hummingbird, the world's smallest bird, weighs about 2 gm.
2. Sonu Nigam sang the title song of *Tees Maar Khan* in fifty-four different voices, though some of them were digitally altered.
3. The word Quark, used to signify the fundamental constituents of matter, was taken from James Joyce's novel *Finnegan's Wake*.
4. Three quarters of the world's total supply of freshwater is frozen in glaciers.
5. Founded in 1829, the Royal Calcutta Golf Course is the oldest of its kind outside the British Isles.
6. The first printing press in India was set up by Jesuit missionaries in Goa in 1556.
7. As a tribute to the great batsman Sachin Tendulkar, Kalimullah Khan, a farmer from Uttar Pradesh, named a variety of mango after him.
8. The human heart starts beating at twenty-one days after conception.
9. Rabindranath Tagore's elder brother, Jyotirindranath Tagore, built a house on Ranchi's Morhabadi Hill, which is now affectionately called the Tagore Hill.

10. Gerontology is the study of old age, the process of ageing, and the particular problems of old people.
11. The coconut gets its name from the Spanish and Portuguese words meaning 'monkey face'.
12. Safdarjung's Tomb is the last enclosed garden tomb in Delhi in the tradition of Humayun's Tomb. The tomb was built for Safdarjung, the last prime minister of Muhammad Shah.

LANGUAGE AND LITERATURE

1. Think differently! Which part of a mechanical watch sounds like it had a previous owner?
2. Who wrote *Ritusamhara* and *Meghaduta*?
3. If you put on jeans or a shirt, what is the correct term for putting on perfume?
4. Which work is often referred to as the fifth veda?
5. Which word would describe what limericks, haikus, sonnets and ballads are?
6. Who wrote a collection of poems called *Kaidi Kaviraj Ki Kundalian*?
7. The Hitopadesha collection of stories is based on which ancient book?
8. Which world famous magician shares his name with the title character of a Charles Dickens novel?
9. Which author's first novel is titled *The Room on the Roof*?
10. Work out the four-letter name of this animal. The first two letters make a verb. The first three an Indian state. The last three a cereal plant and the last two a preposition.
11. With which religion would you associate the Tripitakas?

12. What word links the following: a mountain range in southwest Turkey and the second sign of the Western zodiac?

13. Which author's collection of short stories titled *Soz-e-Watan* in Urdu was banned by the British as it was regarded seditious?

14. What is the difference between 'explode' and 'implode'?

15. In nursery rhymes, what did Little Bo Peep lose?

16. In which book, written by Jules Verne and published in 1870, were submarines spoken of long before their invention?

17. From which two Greek letters is the word 'alphabet' derived?

18. Which play by Shakespeare about a Danish prince whose uncle murders the prince's father, marries his mother, and claims the throne also means a settlement smaller than a village?

19. Which Indian writer founded in 1946 the fine arts magazine *Marg*?

20. Find one word which connects a household electrical appliance, a type of golf club and an element with the symbol Fe.

21. John Huffam were the middle names of which author?

22. Which novel did D.H. Lawrence describe as 'An epic of the sea such as no man has equalled'?

23. Which fictional character written by Mark Twain was looked after by Widow Douglas?

24. What word would link a person who is mean with money, Donald Duck's uncle, and a character in Charles Dickens's *A Christmas Carol*?

25. In which famous novel by Harriet Beecher Stowe would you find the characters Tom, Topsy and Eva?
26. The first sentence of which novel is 'It is a truth universally acknowledged, that a single man in possession of a good fortune, must be in want of a wife'?
27. Which four-letter word would link the following: a financial establishment, the area near a river and a mound of a particular substance?
28. Which famous couple wrote the books *Between Hope and History* and *It Takes a Village* respectively?
29. Who wrote *A Brief History of Time*?
30. The first draft of L. Frank Baum's famous book was originally called *The Emerald City*. What is it known as today?
31. Which author played the role of Saila in the 1985 film *Massey Sahib*?
32. Who is a ghostwriter?
33. What do you call a person or an animal having a congenital absence of pigment in the hair, eyes and skin?
34. Which punctuation mark is derived from a Greek word meaning 'limb or clause'?
35. According to a novel by Alexander Dumas, how do we know Edmond Dantes better?
36. The word 'Yule' refers to which well-known festival?
37. Which five-letter word means 'to catch animals illegally' or 'cook an egg without its shell in or over boiling water'?
38. Which naturalist is the author of *Tree Tops*?
39. According to *The Thousand and One Nights*, what was Aladdin's nationality?

40. If you were reading the teachings of Viswambhara Mishra, whose work would you be reading?
41. Which author's work, *How Much Land Does a Man Need*, did James Joyce call 'the greatest story that the literature of the world knows'?
42. *Rasidi Ticket* was the autobiography of which famous author?
43. 'Never tickle a sleeping dragon' is the motto of which fictional school?
44. In the Mahabharata, who was known as Gangeya?
45. Which American author was the sixth child of John Marshall and Jane Clemens?
46. Which Shakespearean character was safe until Birnam Wood came to Dunsinane Castle?
47. In *Oliver Twist*, Fagin was a master trainer of which criminal profession?
48. On which author's story is the 2003 film *Pinjar* based?
49. In literature, A.A. Milne is well known for creating popular stories of Christopher Robin and his toy bear. Name the bear.
50. Which book, published in 1852, was smuggled into Russia in Yiddish to evade Czarist censors?

Answers on pages 141–143

SPOT THE ANSWER 1

1. Which of these notes does not have the special feature that helps the visually impaired to identify the denomination?
   a. ₹10
   b. ₹20
   c. ₹50

2. The name of which of these cities literally means 'the city of cut-stone'?
   a. Nalanda
   b. Kalinga
   c. Taxila

3. From the tears of which god is the rudraksha tree believed to have originated?
   a. Vishnu
   b. Shiva
   c. Brahma

4. Rudolf Diels was the first head of the organization initially called Department 1A of the Prussian State Police. By what name was it later known?

a. CIA
b. KGB
c. Gestapo

5. In which Indian state did the Kalamkari art form originate?
a. West Bengal
b. Andhra Pradesh
c. Orissa

6. During the early 1900s, who became the guardian of the ruler of Travancore?
a. Raja Rao
b. Raja Ravi Varma
c. Raja Rammohan Roy

7. Which of these rivers features in *The Adventures of Tom Sawyer*?
a. Nile
b. Amazon
c. Mississippi

8. If the president of India wishes to resign from his post, whom should he/she address the letter of resignation to?
a. The vice president
b. The prime minister
c. The army chief

9. In Japanese, the name of which martial art form literally means 'way of harmonizing energy'?

   a. Tae kwon do
   b. Kung fu
   c. Aikido

10. What kind of animal is the 'kulan' that is generally found in the Gobi Desert?
   a. Wild camel
   b. Wild ass
   c. Antelope

11. Which accessory could you buy using the measuring instrument Brannock device?
   a. Ring
   b. Shoe
   c. Necktie

12. Who was independent India's first education minister?
   a. Maulana Abul Kalam Azad
   b. Lala Lajpat Rai
   c. Vallabhbhai Patel

13. If you were living in Srinagar and a snowfall blocked your door, which common kitchen item would you use to unblock it?
   a. Salt
   b. Sugar
   c. Pepper

14. Which of these is the usual cause of devastating tidal waves called tsunamis?
   a. Solar eclipses
   b. Strong underwater earthquakes
   c. Melting of icebergs

15. According to Hindu mythology, which incarnation of Lord Vishnu killed all the male Kshatriyas on Earth, twenty-one times in succession?
    a. Parashurama
    b. Kurma
    c. Krishna

16. Which Indian was nominated for the Nobel Peace Prize in 1937, 1938, 1939, 1947 and 1948 but was never awarded the prize?
    a. Mahatma Gandhi
    b. Jawaharlal Nehru
    c. J.R.D. Tata

17. Which musical instrument is made up of the tumba, tabli and gulu?
    a. Tabla
    b. Sitar
    c. Piano

18. What is the main ingredient of shahi tukda?
    a. Bread pieces
    b. Cottage cheese
    c. Vermicelli

19. According to the nursery rhyme, after Jack fell down, whom did he run to for assistance?
    a. Old Man Top
    b. Old Dame Dob
    c. Jill

20. In the Lok Sabha, which state has the highest number
    of seats?
    a. Maharashtra
    b. Uttar Pradesh
    c. West Bengal

21. Which cricketer's first daughter is named after the
    Australian city Sydney?
    a. Shane Warne
    b. Brian Lara
    c. Mark Waugh

22. Which of these is generally used to sterilize drinking
    water and to purify swimming pools?
    a. Iodine
    b. Chlorine
    c. Potassium

23. Who among these has represented India in rugby?
    a. Ashutosh Gowariker
    b. Rahul Bose
    c. Farhan Akhtar

24. In a calendar year, which is the only 31-day month
    that is followed by another 31-day month?
    a. June
    b. July
    c. August

25. On a Param Vir Chakra medal, the words 'Param Vir
    Chakra' are written in two languages. Which two?

   a.   Hindi and English
   b.   Hindi and Sanskrit
   c.   Hindi and Tamil

26. Which mountain range is divided into the Sambhar–Sirohi range and the Sambhar–Khetri range?
   a.   Aravalli
   b.   Satpura
   c.   Himalayas

27. In the Mahabharata, Duryodhana cried like which creature when he was born?
   a.   Ass
   b.   Horse
   c.   Elephant

28. The principal seat of the authority of the Chandela rulers is a world heritage site. Name it.
   a.   Khajuraho
   b.   Mahabalipuram
   c.   Hampi

29. Which Indian dance form traces its traditions to the Mahari, the Gotipua and the Bandha Nritya traditions?
   a.   Kathak
   b.   Kathakali
   c.   Odissi

30. Which spice is produced by treating the crimson stamen of a flower?

    a. Mace
    b. Turmeric
    c. Saffron

31. What is the surname of Parvati in the Harry Potter series of books?
    a. Patil
    b. Peter
    c. Sarawati

32. Who advises the Government of India on legal matters?
    a. Attorney General
    b. Speaker of the Lok Sabha
    c. Governor of Reserve Bank of India

33. Who was the first cricket umpire to officiate in three successive World Cup final matches?
    a. Steve Bucknor
    b. David Shepherd
    c. Dickie Bird

34. Which is the only continent where owls are not found in the wild?
    a. Australia
    b. Antarctica
    c. Europe

35. In which film has Michelle McNally's story been memorably told?
    a. *Black*

   b. *Family*
   c. *Hum Tum*

36. In the abbreviation ATM, what does M stand for?
   a. Machine
   b. Mobile
   c. Money

37. Which embroidery are 'Dhanya Bagh', 'Motia Bagh' and 'Satrang Bagh' types of?
   a. Kantha
   b. Suzni
   c. Phulkari

38. The roads of which Indian Union Territory are based on a unique plan called 7Vs by its original planner?
   a. Pondicherry
   b. Andaman and Nicobar Islands
   c. Chandigarh

39. Kamban, Krittibas and Tulsidas have all written different versions of which work?
   a. The Ramayana
   b. Vedas
   c. Upanishads

40. Which famous author wrote *Euclid and His Modern Rivals*, a rare example of a humorous work concerning mathematics?
   a. Charles Dickens
   b. Mark Twain
   c. Lewis Carroll

41. Who is the author of *Natyashastra*?
    a. Bhasa
    b. Tulsidas
    c. Bharata Muni

42. With which food item does the legendary king, who presides over the carnival in Goa, share his name?
    a. Momo
    b. Thukpa
    c. Sushi

43. Who wrote the novel *Kidnapped*?
    a. R.L. Stevenson
    b. Charles Dickens
    c. Enid Blyton

44. Who was the first woman to be appointed the governor of Uttar Pradesh?
    a. Sucheta Kripalani
    b. Sarojini Naidu
    c. Vijaya Lakshmi Pandit

45. Against which team did the Indian women's cricket team play its first Test match?
    a. England
    b. Australia
    c. West Indies

46. Which bird varieties are the ivory-billed, the acorn and the great spotted?
    a. Pigeons

b. Woodpeckers
c. Emus

47. Who served as the prime minister of India for seventeen years?
   a. Jawaharlal Nehru
   b. Indira Gandhi
   c. P.V. Narasimha Rao

48. The name of which Indian percussion instrument literally means 'made of clay'?
   a. Mridangam
   b. Shehnai
   c. Santoor

49. What was adopted on 26 November 1949, but came into force on 26 January 1950?
   a. The Constitution of India
   b. The National Flag
   c. The National Emblem

50. Which water body is called Khalije Fars in Persian and Bahr Fars in Arabic?
   a. Persian Gulf
   b. Gulf of Oman
   c. Red Sea

Answers on pages 143–144

MYTHOLOGY

1. According to Hindu mythology, who was the eldest son of Vishravas and Kaikasi?
2. Which Hindu god is called Vigneshwara as he removes obstacles?
3. In the Ramayana, whom did Anusuya, the wife of Atri, give an ointment to that would keep her beautiful forever?
4. With which Hindu god would you associate the Tandava dance?
5. Who cursed Krishna that he would be killed by trickery?
6. According to mythology, who lifted the Govardhana mountain?
7. Which deity is credited with teaching Ayurveda to Sushruta?
8. According to Hindu mythology, which snake killed Parikshit?
9. In the Mahabharata, who built the lac palace?
10. Lord Krishna was born when Vishnu sent a black hair into Devaki's womb. Who was born when he sent a white hair into Rohini's womb?

11. Which part of Achilles' body was vulnerable (his weak point)?
12. Which deity is also called Mahisasurmardini?
13. Who married the demoness Hidimbi?
14. Who was the commander of the Kaurava forces after the fall of Bhishma?
15. Who gave Parashurama his axe?
16. According to Hindu mythology, who is often referred to as the 'Adi kavi'?
17. According to Hindu mythology, who built the palace of Yama?
18. In Norse mythology, Mjölnir is the hammer of which god?
19. Who was killed by Lakshmana before he could perform a yagna that would make him invulnerable?
20. In Greek mythology, by what name were Medusa, Stheno (the strong) and Euryale (the wide leaping) collectively known?
21. Which mischievous Greek god had the horns, legs, and ears of a goat?
22. What was the original name of the Mahabharata composed by Vyasa?
23. In Greek mythology, who was the strongest mortal ever?
24. In the Mahabharata, which great sage was the spiritual teacher of the Pandavas and the Kauravas?
25. According to the Greek poet Homer, heaven was located on the summit of which mountain?
26. What profession did Arjuna assume at Raja Virata's court?
27. Who taught Bhima the use of the mace?

28. The head of the Egyptian deity Anubis resembled the head of which animal?
29. In Hindu mythology, who designed Yama's palace?
30. The Pandavas spent one year in disguise at King Virata's court. What profession did Sahadeva take up there?
31. After which goddess in Norse mythology is Friday named?
32. Which god rides an elephant called Airavata?
33. Zeus was the father of the Greek Muses. Who was their mother?
34. Which rakshasa took the form of a golden deer to lure Lakshmana away, leaving Sita unprotected?
35. Who became the king of Lanka after Ravana was defeated and killed?
36. Which legendary British king was the son of King Uther Pendragon?
37. In Hindu mythology, who made the bow called Vijaya and gave it to Indra?
38. Which Pandava was also known as Dhananjaya?
39. In the Ramayana, which rakshasa was known as Jaya and served as Vishnu's gatekeeper at Vaikuntha?
40. If Lord Shiva's abode is Kailash, who stays at Vaikuntha?
41. Which planet was named by the Romans after their god of war because of its red, blood-like colour?
42. In the Ramayana, whose wife was Srutakirti?
43. Who was the commander of the Pandava forces during the battle of Kurukshetra?
44. In Hindu mythology, which goddess lodged herself on Kumbhakarna's tongue and made him ask for the boon of sleep from Brahma?

45. According to Hindu mythology, which famous sage gave the impetus to Valmiki to compose the Ramayana?
46. In the Mahabharata, who killed Shakuni during the Kurukshetra war?
47. Which Greek nymph's hopeless love for Narcissus made her fade away until only her voice remained?
48. In the Mahabharata, who was Ved Vyasa's mother?
49. In Greek mythology, who opened a box and set free all evils?
50. According to mythology, what is the name of Krishna's chakra?

Answers on pages 144–146

MIXED BAG 1

1. In 1865, the first edition of which book by an English mathematician was withdrawn because of bad printing?
2. Which famous Kathak dancer founded a dance school named Kalashram?
3. What in India is used in the following sizes: 225 x 150 mm for motorcars and 150 x 100 mm for tables?
4. In the US, which breed of dog has served as the firefighters' mascot?
5. Of what are sizes 137 x 63 mm, 147 x 73 mm, 157 x 73 mm, 167 x 73 mm, 177 x 73 mm important features?
6. The name of which shiny mineral comes from Latin, literally meaning 'crumb'?
7. This planet was predicted by a Frenchman called Le Verrier and an Englishman named John Adams. (The French wanted to name the planet Le Verrier in his honour.) Which planet are we talking about?
8. The Apatanis are traditionally one of the most advanced weavers of which northeastern Indian state?
9. Fill in the blank to complete this Albert Einstein quote: '_____ is more difficult than Physics.'
10. In India, which monument is seen on the reverse side of the ₹50 note?

11. Whose alter-ego was Pandit Gangadhar Vidyadhar Mayadhar Omkarnath Shastri?
12. In India, which intricate shadow-work embroidery uses white yarn on colourless muslins called 'tanzeb'?
13. In which category did M.S. Subbulakshmi win the Magsaysay Award in 1974?
14. Which musical instrument was referred to as Shata-Tantri Veena in ancient times?
15. How is peppermint camphor better known?
16. Who was president of the Indian Constituent Assembly between 1946–49?
17. Which Greek goddess shares her name with a part of the eye?
18. In 1963, John Wisden & Co. donated the Wisden Trophy that is awarded to the winner of the Test series between which two teams?
19. Which landmark in Uttar Pradesh was built in 1784 as a famine relief project?
20. Name the antibiotic also known as the first 'wonder drug'.
21. In USA, the Newbery Medal is awarded for contribution to which form of literature?
22. Which term, also meaning 'to fix firmly and deeply in a surrounding mass', was used to describe journalists who travelled with allied army formations during the Gulf War of 2003?
23. In 1943, the government of which country issued Azad Hind postage stamps for Subhas Chandra Bose?
24. In India, if a woman can vote at the age of eighteen, at what minimum age can a man vote?
25. What is the first hour of every sitting of the Lok Sabha called?

26. In Japan, what is Bunraku a type of?
27. Which Indian leader lived in a place called Hriday Kunj from 1918 to 1930?
28. In Varanasi, what are Manikarnika, Asi, Man Mandir and Dasaswamedh?
29. In 1860, who established a training school for nurses at St Thomas' Hospital in London?
30. In India, which dynasty issued gold coins for the first time?
31. After whom is the chemical element with atomic number 102 named?
32. Who was the first Indian military officer to be conferred the rank of Field Marshal?
33. The introduction of Assamese as the official language in 1960 was the reason for a movement resulting in the formation of a new state in 1972. Which state are we talking about?
34. Which country is sometimes referred to as 'Chhota Bharat'?
35. According to belief, which precious stone is usually worn on one's hand to prevent epilepsy?
36. In Germany, this sign is called the 'Hakenkreuz'. What is it called in India?
37. In the first part of which famous work is the main character generally known as Man-Mountain?
38. Which musician's biography, by Surjit Singh, is called *Woodwinds of Change*?
39. In anthropology, which term is used to describe a member of any human group whose adult males grow to less than 150 cm (59 inches) in average height?

40. Which was the first country to gain independence in the new millennium (2001–02)?
41. Which animal's Swahili name is Kiboko?
42. How many concentric circles would you see on the emblem of the United Nations?
43. Who is the first batsman to appear on the cover of Wisden Cricketers' Almanack 2003 in its 140-year history?
44. Which tourist attraction in Delhi, built in the memory of King Chandra, has not yet rusted?
45. What is the common name for a form of 'seborrheic dermatitis' that affects the scalp?
46. 'Ball', also known as 'globe', and 'bead' are forms of which natural phenomenon?
47. In war parlance, which three words do you use for the stretch of ground between two enemy lines?
48. Who was the first Communist chief minister in India?
49. Which part of the Earth did Roald Amundsen visit for the first time?
50. Which Indian town was once divided into Ville Noire and Ville Blanche?

Answers on pages 146–148

FUN FACTS 2

1. During the 1870s, a large swarm of locusts, 300 miles long and 100 miles wide, migrated through the US Great Plains.

2. Amitabh Bachchan got his first film *Saat Hindustani* on the recommendation of the then prime minister Indira Gandhi, as he was a friend of her son Rajiv.

3. Winnie the Pooh was named after a real bear called Winnie at the London Zoo.

4. The Sundarbans, covering 10,000 sq km of mangrove forest and water, is part of the world's largest delta formed by three great rivers—the Ganges, Brahmaputra and Meghna, which converge on the Bengal Basin.

5. During the Soviet era, the Dynamo Moscow Football Club was sponsored by the Russian secret service organization, KGB.

6. Shams al-Dīn Iltutmish, the third and greatest Delhi sultan of the Slave dynasty, was sold into slavery. Later, he married the daughter of his master, Qutub-ud-Din Aibak, whom he succeeded to the throne of Delhi, in 1211.

7. Jackfruit is said to be the largest tree-borne fruit in the world.
8. Krishnattam, a folk theatre of Kerala, came into existence in the middle of the seventeenth century CE, under the patronage of King Mahadeva of Calicut. The episodes are based on the life of Lord Krishna—his birth, childhood pranks and various deeds.
9. Organized in July every year, 'Van Mahotsav' is a week-long tree planting festival in India.
10. The Durand Line, established in 1863, demarcating the lands of Afghanistan and British India, now marks the border between Afghanistan and Pakistan.
11. The name Varanasi originated from two rivers, Varana and Asi, arising from the right and left leg of Bhagavan Yogasayi, making it a holy place.
12. During World War II, a set of five 500 lb bombs struck the Centre Court of Wimbledon, resulting in huge damages to its original galleries.

WHAT'S THE QUESTION 2

1. Wife of King Dasharatha, she was the mother of Bharata
2. A stretch of salt water separated from the sea by a coral reef
3. Anne Sullivan's famous deaf and blind pupil
4. This trio is based in Townsville.
5. A mounted military servant of a lord (Hint: Middle Ages)
6. Steam bath of Finnish origin
7. He is known as Qaid-i-Azam in Pakistan.
8. Indian term for approximately 11.6 gm
9. An antibiotic discovered by Alexander Fleming in 1929
10. His parents were killed by Lord Voldemort.
11. Diagrammatic representation of a sequence of events (Hint: Computers)
12. This American track and field athlete was the hero of the 1936 Berlin Olympics.
13. This Indian festival's name means 'bond of protection'.
14. Comes from the Norwegian word meaning 'snowshoe'
15. It is the largest organ in the human body accounting for 16 per cent of the body weight.

16. In Greek legend, the most beautiful woman of Greece who was abducted by Paris.
17. Fannings and dust are forms of this beverage.
18. The largest brackish water lake in Orissa
19. Victoria Beckham was a part of this pop group.
20. The Greek word for 'chief builder'
21. The instrument panel in a vehicle or aircraft
22. Spring bulb with trumpet-shaped yellow flowers
23. Tibetan dumplings stuffed with vegetables or meat
24. He won the Battle of Waterloo in 1815.
25. It is also known as the All India War Memorial.
26. The change between the solid and the gaseous phases of matter, with no intermediate liquid stage.
27. It is called the reindeer in Europe.
28. This fabric was introduced by Sir H.B. Lumsden and W. Hodson in 1848 for British colonial troops in India.
29. The first Indian president to die in office.
30. Batted full sixty overs scoring just 36 runs in an ODI
31. A God-fearing person much loved by George Shelby
32. In 1900, this politician published his only novel, *Savrola*.
33. Hedwig
34. This breed of dog was often referred to as 'sleeve dog' as it was carried by Chinese royalty in the sleeves of their robes.
35. The resistance that one surface or object encounters when moving over another
36. He made a match-winning score of 281 runs against Australia in Kolkata in 2001.
37. US president who approved the dropping of atomic bombs on Japan

38. Shamshabad Airport or Rajiv Gandhi International Airport
39. According to UNESCO, she is the most translated woman author in the world.
40. The German Secret State Police during World War II
41. 1984 Nobel Peace Prize winner, 1985 Bishop of Johannesburg
42. The Greeks referred to this planet as 'Apollo' in the morning, and 'Hermes' in the evening.
43. Two theories that relate matter, space and time (Hint: Einstein)
44. Bourbon, Java, Bourbon-like and Mexican are its types.
45. Parvati and Padma Patil are characters created by her.
46. Built in 1591 to commemorate the end of the plague
47. This comic-strip character is the personal safety mascot of NASA astronauts.
48. This cricketer replaced the platypus on Australia's twenty-cent coin in 2001.
49. Triton
50. This book consists of 1,028 hymns dedicated to various gods.

Answers on pages 148–149

GEOGRAPHY

1. The name of which African country with its capital at Cairo ends with the letter 'T'?
2. What is the colour of the disc on the National Flag of Bangladesh?
3. Which mythical animal appears on the flag of Bhutan?
4. Along which river is Dibrugarh located?
5. Which mountain peak is called Chomolungma in Tibetan?
6. Which former Indian princely state lies between Assam, Mizoram and Bangladesh?
7. Which famous landmark in Sydney is affectionately nicknamed 'the coathanger'?
8. 'Thou art the ruler of the minds' (when translated) is the opening line of the National Anthem of which country?
9. Which state of the USA lies at the extreme northwest of the North American continent and is the largest peninsula in the western hemisphere?
10. In terms of average elevation, which is the highest continent in the world?
11. Which European country occupies the peninsula of Jutland, and is an archipelago of more than 400 islands?

12. Which is the most plentiful element in the Earth's atmosphere?
13. The name of which capital city means 'top of the hill'?
14. What were sometimes called 'dissected maps' and were used to teach geography in England?
15. Lao is the official language of which Asian country?
16. In which state is Jaldapara Wildlife Sanctuary located?
17. Name the second largest US state in terms of area. (Hint: Austin is the capital and Houston is its largest city.)
18. Which two African countries end with the letters 'YA'?
19. Oman ends with the word 'Man'. Which country in Asia ends with the word 'Men'.
20. Which seven-letter word connects the surname of a cartoon character and a desert in Australia?
21. Which city is the winter capital of Jammu and Kashmir?
22. Which mountain peak is locally called Dapsang or Chogori?
23. Name the only independent country in the world beginning with the letter 'Q'.
24. Which British overseas territory is only 6.5 sq km in area?
25. The Arabs refer to which country as Serendib?
26. Which country is divided into two parts called Thrace and Anatolia?
27. Two Indian states have the same initials and end with the same seven-letter words. Name them.
28. Other than India, which Asian country begins with the letters 'Ind' and ends with 'Ia'?

29. Gandhinagar lies on the right bank of which river?
30. What is the name of Assam's only hill station?
31. Jaipur is called the Pink City. Which city in Rajasthan is called the Blue City?
32. Which Indian tourist attraction, built in a short span of hundred years (950–1050 CE), derives its name from the prevalence of date palms in the area?
33. This Indian state was under colonial rule for 450 years and was a Union Territory for twenty-six years. Name it.
34. If you were admiring the Olive Ridley sea turtles on the Gahirmatha Beach, in which Indian state would you be?
35. If you were interested in visiting the place where Babur fought the First Battle of Panipat, which state would you have to visit?
36. Who erected the Tower of Victory to commemorate his victory over Mahmud Khilji of Malwa in 1440?
37. Which Mughal emperor gave Ahmedabad the title 'Gardabad' meaning 'City of Dust'?
38. If you visited the Karni Mata Temple at Bikaner in Rajasthan, which animal or animals would you see being worshipped?
39. Name the international township and study centre named after Sri Aurobindo Ghose in Pondicherry.
40. The name of which state of India literally means 'Abode of Clouds'?
41. Which city in Kerala is referred to as the 'Venice of the East' by travellers across the world?
42. In which Indian state is the Kalatop Wildlife Sanctuary located?

43. If you wanted to visit the Black Forest, which country would you visit?
44. In northeastern Wyoming, USA, there is a tower of volcanic rock that rises 600 feet from the hills bordering the Belle Fourche river. What is it called?
45. It lies in Australia and rises 335 metres abruptly from the sand dune plains, about 450 km from Alice Springs. It is perhaps the world's largest monolith. What is it?
46. Which peak is called Kumbhkaran Langur in Nepali?
47. Ankara is the capital of which country?
48. In which Indian city would you be if you got down at the Egmore railway station?
49. Which acclaimed site/creation in Chandigarh, built by Nek Chand, consists of art objects fashioned from industrial and urban waste?
50. Which Asian mountain is also known as the Savage Mountain?

Answers on pages 150–151

ENTERTAINMENT

1. Which comic-strip character gets his powers from the Earth's yellow sun?
2. Which Indian cricketer acted in the film *Savli Premachi*?
3. Which actor is the son of actor Pankaj Kapoor?
4. What connects the bands Boyzone, Backstreet Boys, Code Red, 98 Degrees and Boys II Men?
5. Which was the first film to win the Oscar for Best Animated Feature Film?
6. In the world of music, what would you associate with Shellac, Vulcanite, Columbia, Edison Diamond and Vinyl?
7. About whom did President Jimmy Carter say: 'He is an ambassador of goodwill and a peacemaker who speaks the universal language of friendship'?
8. Who does the cartoon cat Sylvester always try to catch and eat, but is foiled by the bulldog Hector?
9. Popeye has an anchor tattooed on his arm. What tattoo do his four nephews have?
10. Supremo, a famous comic-strip character of the 1980s, was styled after which Hindi film actor?

11. Elvis Presley died on 16 August 1977. Twenty years later, which Pakistani qawwali singer died on the same day?
12. Which was the first film in the history of Indian cinema to celebrate a silver jubilee initial release at over 100 theatres across India?
13. Which Indi-pop singer was born Sujata, and was known for her hit 'Made in India'?
14. Which cartoon duo's first cartoon together was called *Puss Gets the Boot*?
15. In which Indian city did Tintin stop over in the book *Tintin in Tibet*?
16. What was the name of the druid in Asterix comics?
17. Who was the subject of the 1987 television serial called *Crossbow*?
18. In films, which character had a chimpanzee called Cheetah as a companion?
19. Which Irish pop band connects: Sinead O'Carroll, Lindsay Armaou, Edele Lynch and Keavy Lynch?
20. In the Scooby-Doo gang, which character, portrayed in the film by Linda Cardellini, cannot see without her spectacles?
21. In which Tintin adventure do Tintin and Captain Haddock arrive at Cointrin Airport in Geneva by a Swissair flight?
22. In the world of entertainment, how is Enrique Martin Morales better known?
23. In the Asterix comics, which character is called Assurancetourix in French?
24. The Brahma Bull symbol is associated with which professional wrestler?

25. Which board game is played with 100 tiles on 225 squares?
26. Who was Govinda's *jodidar* (partner) in Jodi No. 1?
27. What is the name of the adventure that appears in the first Asterix book?
28. Dr Doom and Dr Octopus are two enemies of which comic hero?
29. What was Kallu's profession in the 2002 film *Makdee*?
30. Who played the role of Miss Hawa Hawai in the 1998 film *Chhota Chetan*?
31. How are Chance Furlong and Jake Clawson better known?
32. In the 1986 film *Bhagwaan Dada*, which later-day superstar played the character called Govinda?
33. Which singer is famous for his song 'Bulla Ki Jana Main Kaun'?
34. In which 2005 Ram Gopal Varma film would you meet Subhas, Shankar and Vishnu Nagare?
35. Of which music group are Pakistan-based Bilal Maqsood and Faisal Kapadia members?
36. How is the late singer/actor Abhas Kumar Ganguly better known?
37. Which character did Amitabh Bachchan play in the film *Amar Akbar Anthony*?
38. What instrument does Ustad Hafiz Ali Khan's famous son play?
39. Kudiyattam, performed by the Cakkayars of Kerala, is the only surviving theatre form in which language?
40. *Meenaxi: A Tale of Three Cities* is the second full-length feature film by which famous Indian?
41. Which actress is married to Ajay Devgan?

42. For which film did Adrien Brody win the Best Actor Oscar in 2003?
43. Which music duo are the sons of music director Chitragupta?
44. Which sitarist's debut film is *Dance Like a Man*?
45. With which dance form is Kelucharan Mahapatra associated?
46. Who was the last film director to be awarded the Bharat Ratna?
47. Who invited Atomba Singh to teach Manipuri dancing in Bengal in the 1920s?
48. If you used your hand to play a 'harmonium', what would you use to play a 'harmonica'?
49. If Scotland is known for its bagpipes, what musical instrument is the national symbol of Ireland?
50. In a theatre, what is the name given to the part of the stage in front of the curtains, stretching into the audience area?

Answers on pages 151–153

SPOT THE ANSWER 2

1. According to Hindu mythology, which was the second of the four yugas?
    a. Kali yuga
    b. Treta yuga
    c. Dvapara yuga

2. Which battle of Panipat was fought in the eighteenth century?
    a. First
    b. Second
    c. Third

3. The life of which deity makes up the most common theme of Pahadi paintings?
    a. Buddha
    b. Narada
    c. Krishna

4. By what Indian name is 'sweet golden yoghurt' better known?
    a. Shrikhand
    b. Kheer
    c. Paneer

5. Which Nobel Laureate's autobiography is *Freedom in Exile*?
   a. Nelson Mandela
   b. Dalai Lama
   c. Aung San Suu Kyi

6. What fraction of the Rajya Sabha retires every second year?
   a. Half
   b. One-third
   c. One-fourth

7. A Rest of the World vs MCC match played at Lord's in 1987 was which Indian cricketer's last first-class match?
   a. Kapil Dev
   b. Ravi Shastri
   c. Sunil Gavaskar

8. Which animal's extinct species are Javan, Bali and Caspian?
   a. Elephant
   b. Deer
   c. Tiger

9. Who wrote the novels *Sevasadan*, *Rangamanch*, *Gaban*, *Nirmala* and *Godan*?
   a. Munshi Premchand
   b. Amrita Pritam
   c. Mahasweta Devi

10. Which musical instrument did Guru Nanak's friend and companion Mardana play?
    a. Sitar
    b. Tanpura
    c. Rabab

11. In 1982, the advent of colour television coincided with which event in India?
    a. First General Elections
    b. First Census
    c. Asian Games inauguration

12. In which of these places is the famous Cellular Jail located?
    a. Andaman and Nicobar Islands
    b. Kerala
    c. Karnataka

13. In the Ramayana, who is Rama's sister?
    a. Urmila
    b. Kanta
    c. Shanta

14. Which is the largest and heaviest internal organ within the human body?
    a. Liver
    b. Heart
    c. Lung

15. In batik method of dyeing, patterned parts are traditionally covered with which substance so that

they do not receive colour?
a. Sugar
b. Wax
c. Salt

16. Penne, bow and fusilli are different kinds of which tasty food item?
a. Ice cream
b. Cheese
c. Pasta

17. Which work by Kalidasa recounts the legend of Rama's ancestors and descendants?
a. *Meghadutam*
b. *Vikramorvashi*
c. *Raghuvansham*

18. In Karnataka, a yakshagana performance starts and ends with a prayer to which god?
a. Ganesha
b. Rama
c. Indra

19. In which game is the term 'fluke' used?
a. Billiards
b. Football
c. Hockey

20. Which animal's smallest specimen is Pudu?
a. Dog
b. Deer
c. Cheetah

21. In ancient Rome, the warning 'cave canem' was meant for people to beware of which animal?
    a. Dog
    b. Cat
    c. Eagle

22. Cinema Ghar in Hyderabad mainly houses paintings of which Indian artist?
    a. Satish Gujral
    b. M.F. Hussain
    c. Jamini Roy

23. Which art form of Persia was introduced in Rajasthan under the patronage of Maharaja Ram Singhji?
    a. Batik
    b. Filigree
    c. Blue pottery

24. Which Indian state was known as Lushai Hills District and was a part of Assam?
    a. Meghalaya
    b. Mizoram
    c. Nagaland

25. In Hindu mythology, who among these was born in Mithila?
    a. Draupadi
    b. Madri
    c. Sita

26. In the eighteenth century, which metal did King Louis

XV of France declare as the only metal fit for a king?
a. Platinum
b. Silver
c. Iron

27. In which Indian state is the Surajkund Crafts Mela held?
a. Punjab
b. Andhra Pradesh
c. Haryana

28. Which nut is attached to a yellow or red pear-shaped false fruit?
a. Almond
b. Cashew nut
c. Walnut

29. For which monument were 20,000 workmen accommodated in a small town named Mumtazabad in the 1630s?
a. Red Fort
b. Taj Mahal
c. Agra Fort

30. Sri Jayawardenepura Kotte is the legislative and judicial capital of which country?
a. Maldives
b. Sri Lanka
c. Seychelles

31. Of which international sporting event were Kaz, Ato and Nik mascots?

    a.   FIFA World Cup 2002
    b.   Winter Olympics 2002
    c.   Summer Olympics 2000

32. Which of these animals holds the record for having the largest brain in the world?
    a.   Sperm whale
    b.   Elephant
    c.   Giraffe

33. Who directed the 2005 film *Iqbal*?
    a.   Nagesh Kukunoor
    b.   Mohit Suri
    c.   Meera Nair

34. If you were playing Scrabble, which letter tile are you likely to encounter the maximum number of times?
    a.   A
    b.   E
    c.   O

35. Complete this Sunderlal Bahuguna phrase which he coined during the Chipko Movement: 'Ecology is permanent _____.'
    a.   Economy
    b.   Sociology
    c.   Biology

36. Who was the first woman to win the Nobel Prize?
    a.   Marie Curie
    b.   Mother Teresa
    c.   Florence Nightingale

37. In the hermitage of which sage was Shakuntala brought up?
    a. Kanva
    b. Agastya
    c. Dronacharya

38. The name of which spice comes from the French word for nail?
    a. Cinnamon
    b. Cardamom
    c. Clove

39. Which instrument inspired the rabab, has a metal fingerboard but no frets, and is played with a pick made of coconut shell?
    a. Sarod
    b. Sitar
    c. Tanpura

40. Which of these herbs, used extensively in Indian cuisine, is referred to as 'dhania' in Hindi?
    a. Coriander
    b. Fenugreek
    c. Asafoetida

41. M.K. Gandhi lived in a farm in South Africa named after a famous Russian novelist. Name the author.
    a. Leo Tolstoy
    b. Mark Twain
    c. Charles Dickens

42. Kisan Ghat is the memorial ground of which famous leader?
    a. Charan Singh
    b. Rajiv Gandhi
    c. Jagjivan Ram

43. In which city can you find the mausoleum of Arjumand Bano Begum?
    a. Delhi
    b. Agra
    c. Aurangabad

44. Which celestial body is most visited by space probes from Earth?
    a. Mars
    b. Moon
    c. Venus

45. In 2008, who was the first Indian actor to receive the prestigious Malaysian title, 'Datuk'?
    a. Aamir Khan
    b. Ajay Devgan
    c. Shah Rukh Khan

46. In which device might you come across a trackball?
    a. TV camera
    b. Computer
    c. Watch

47. What took place in India for the first time in July 1896 at Watson's Hotel in Mumbai?

    a. First Congress annual session
    b. First film screening
    c. First theatre festival

48. Which country's highest peak is Mount Ararat?
    a. China
    b. Turkey
    c. Singapore

49. In the Mahabharata, which grandson of Pandu died in warfare when he was trapped in a 'Chakravyuha'?
    a. Abhimanyu
    b. Prativindhya
    c. Yaudheya

50. In Buddhism, what among these does the 'swastika' signify?
    a. Buddha's feet or footprints
    b. Teachings of Buddha
    c. Signature of Buddha

Answers on pages 153–155

FUN FACTS 3

1. The ancient Egyptians were the first known beekeepers.
2. The Oscar statuette is a knight holding a crusader's sword, standing on a reel of film. The reel features five spokes, signifying the five original branches of the Academy (actors, directors, producers, technicians and writers).
3. Many believe that Winston Churchill was awarded the Nobel Peace Prize, but he was actually awarded the 1953 Nobel Prize in Literature. In fact, Churchill was nominated for both the Literature Prize and the Nobel Peace Prize.
4. According to WHO, globally, over 1 billion people lack access to safe drinking water supplies, while 2.6 billion lack adequate sanitation.
5. In the nineteenth century, the members of Middlesex Cricket Club played a pioneering role in developing modern field hockey as we know it today.
6. In 1638, Shah Jahan transferred his capital from Agra to Delhi and laid the foundations of Shahjahanabad, the seventh city of Delhi.
7. Traditionally, tea is known as kahwa in Kashmir.

8. Pluto's unusual elliptical orbit brings it inside Neptune's orbit for a twenty-year period out of every 248 Earth years. Pluto can never crash into Neptune though, because for every three laps Neptune takes around the sun, Pluto makes two.
9. The person who steers a ship, racing boat or any other boat, is called a coxswain.
10. Jammu and Kashmir is the only Indian state which is exempt from paying the service tax.
11. Kutiyattam, one of the oldest forms of theatre in India, originated in Kerala about 2,000 years ago.
12. Dubai was the first country in the world to clone a camel.

MIXED BAG 2

1. In Yahoo.com, what does 'Y' in Yahoo stand for?
2. If Tiger Woods plays golf, which sport did Fabien Barthez play?
3. Which process, named after a French bacteriologist, prevents liquid food from getting spoilt?
4. Which colour connects traffic lights, pandas and blood cells?
5. If a 'coolie' is a person who carries goods, what kind of creature is a 'collie'?
6. Jatiyo Sangshad is the national Parliament of which country?
7. In 1923, which country was founded by Kemal Ataturk from the Anatolian remains of the Ottoman Empire?
8. Lleyton Hewitt has won twenty-eight singles career titles in which sport?
9. What kind of a creature is a jackdaw?
10. Which country occupies about 85 per cent of the Iberian peninsula?
11. On a computer keyboard, what does 'Esc' stand for?
12. Which sport did Franz Beckenbauer play at the international level for Germany?
13. Who was the youngest winner at Roland Garros

beating the then No.1 Steffi Graf in straight sets in the final in 1990?

14. Who won the Nobel Prize in Physics in 1983 'for his theoretical studies of the physical processes of importance to the structure and evolution of the stars'?

15. In which Indian state is the Manas Wildlife Sanctuary?

16. In computers, expand the abbreviation CAD.

17. Spanning seven countries, which is the longest mountain range in the world?

18. Mats Wilander was a world-class player in which sport?

19. In which Indian state is the Meenakshi Temple located?

20. The Humboldt Current flows by which continent?

21. In India, how many languages are there on the languages panel of contemporary currency notes?

22. Who was the first National Professor of independent India?

23. In which sport did Gurcharan Singh represent India at the 2000 Sydney Olympics?

24. Which world heritage site has caves excavated out of the vertical face of Charanandri Hills?

25. Who was the second wife of King Henry VIII and also the mother of Elizabeth I?

26. The leaves of which tree appear on the flag of the United Nations?

27. Pokhran is in which Indian state?

28. If you were holidaying in Chittagong and Sylhet, in which country would you be?

29. Limba Ram represented India in which sport?

30. Which famous monument in Mumbai, located at the Apollo Bunder, overlooks the Arabian Sea?
31. In which Indian state would you see kurinji flowers that bloom once in twelve years?
32. Which sport did Douglas Jardine play for England?
33. The fourteen coaches of which luxury train are named after former Rajput states?
34. Which raw material is produced by the *Bombyx mori* moth?
35. Give a three-letter word for a large, strong African antelope that has the Afrikaans name 'wildebeest'?
36. What does 'B' stand for in the computer programming language BASIC?
37. Which is the only Olympic sport that begins with the letter 'E'?
38. The name of which popular board game for two to four players comes from the Latin word meaning 'I play'?
39. Which desert formation can be described as 'a crescent-shaped sand dune produced by the action of wind mainly from one direction'?
40. Which item of cutlery with prongs is also something you might come across on the road?
41. On the Internet, give an alternative four-letter word for a portal.
42. Give another name for a Mexican lion or cougar beginning with the letter 'P'.
43. Which US president adopted 'White House' as the official name of the Executive Mansion?
44. Which five-letter word for many dozens is also the word for 'fat and ugly'?

45. In which sport did Billie Jean King win sixty-seven singles titles?
46. What is a single dot on a computer screen called?
47. Which was the first Australian city to host the Olympic Games?
48. Which Indian prime minister's birthday is also celebrated on October 2 every year?
49. Who is the author of the books *The Financial Expert* and *The Guide*?
50. With which nineteenth-century sculptor would you associate *The Thinker*, a statue cast in bronze?

Answers on pages 155–156

HISTORY

1. In which present-day state is the historical site of Haldighati located?
2. In the *Arthashastra*, after which mythological character is Land Tax named?
3. On which famous ship did Nelson die after being victorious at the Battle of Trafalgar?
4. Besides being US presidents, what is common to Abraham Lincoln, James Garfield, William McKinley and John F. Kennedy?
5. Who gave the name Nivedita to Margaret Elizabeth Noble?
6. Sarojini Naidu was the governor of UP. Name her daughter who became the governor of West Bengal.
7. The name of which newspaper founded in 1912 in St Petersburg as an underground newspaper, meant 'truth' in Russian?
8. On 15 September 1935, the black swastika on a white circle with a red background became the National Flag of which country?
9. Which president of India served as the vice-chancellor of Benaras Hindu University between 1939–1948?
10. Who became the president of Argentina after the death of Juan Perón in 1974?

11. Which Indian poet, also known as Bharatendu, is commonly referred to as the 'Father of Modern Hindi'?
12. Robert Clive fought Siraj-ud-Daula in the Battle of Plassey in 1757. In which present-day Indian state is Plassey located?
13. Who founded the first school of Mughal painting?
14. Who started the Khudai Khidmatgar movement?
15. Which kingdom was founded by Hasan Gangu in 1347?
16. Who led the fifteen-day long Salt Satyagraha March in Tamil Nadu from Trichy to Vedaranyam on 13 April 1930?
17. Which country was Herodotus referring to when he said: 'There is no country that possesses so many wonders, nor any, that such a number of works that defy description'?
18. In Indian history, what was held at these four places: Rajagriha, Vaishali, Pataliputra and Kundalavahana?
19. Name the epidemic that broke out in Europe in the 1300s and got its name from the black spots that it produced on the victims's bodies.
20. In the fifteenth century, Ivan the Great unified Russia after freeing it from which people? (Hint: Their name sounds like a tooth disease.)
21. During World War II, who offered his people only 'blood, toil, tears and sweat' as they struggled to keep their freedom?
22. In 1600, which queen of England sent a Charter granting the English East India Company the monopoly of trade for fifteen years in India?

23. Which war ended at 11 a.m. on the eleventh day of the eleventh month in 1918?
24. Which leader, born in Braunau am Inn, twice failed to secure entry to the Academy of Fine Arts?
25. Charles Conrad was the third and Alan Bean the fourth. Who were the first two?
26. Name the teacher turned freedom fighter who fought the Italians in Libya and earned the nickname 'Lion of the Desert'?
27. Which ruler's original name was Temüjin?
28. Which famous Italian artist was born on 6 March 1475 in the village of Caprese, Italy? (Hint: He attracted the attention of Lorenzo de Medici.)
29. Which Mughal emperor wrote poetry under the pen name 'Zafar'?
30. Akbar had three main ways of extending his kingdom. Wars were one, treaties were another. What was the third?
31. From which historically important structure did Nadir Shah take the peacock throne?
32. On 12 December 1899, which British prime minister, while working as a war correspondent, escaped from Boer captivity by climbing over the wall of the States Model School in Pretoria?
33. What, according to Mahatma Gandhi, was the 'sun of the village solar system'?
34. Which capital city was formerly called Christiania?
35. In the legend of King Arthur, what was the 'holy grail' that his knights tried hard to find?
36. Whose last words were: 'Go on. Get out. Last words are for fools who haven't said enough'?

37. Who was the first woman to be elected fellow of the Royal Statistical Society in 1860 because of her contribution to army statistics?
38. In 1569 who did Haji Begum build a tomb for?
39. Vatsaraja, Nagabhatta II and Mihir Bhoja belonged to which dynasty from the fifth to the ninth century?
40. Who was the most famous son of Putlibai of Porbandar?
41. Who was the first non-Indian president of the Indian National Congress?
42. In 1964, when Pope Paul VI came to India, he gave his ceremonial limousine to this lady who was born in Skopje in 1910. Who was this well-known lady?
43. Who built the Alai Minar, an incomplete tower next to the Qutb Minar?
44. Which famous Indian drafted the first petitions sent by Indians to a South African legislature in 1894?
45. Who was the famous father of Harilal, Manilal, Ramlal and Devdas?
46. With which European revolution in 1789 is the ideology 'Liberty, Equality and Fraternity' associated?
47. Who defeated Humayun at the Battle of Chausa in 1539?
48. Which Mughal emperor initially ruled under the regency of Bairam Khan?
49. The courtesan Amrapali was a devotee of which famous religious leader?
50. Who founded the Afsharid dynasty that ruled Persia in the eighteenth century?

Answers on pages 156–158

WHAT'S THE QUESTION 3

1. The Enid Blyton character who lives in a toadstool on the edge of the Enchanted Wood.
2. This city in Madhya Pradesh is a site for the Kumbh Mela.
3. The flag of this country features the words 'Ordem e Progresso'.
4. Queen who ruled Great Britain and Ireland between 1837 and 1901
5. The Cholas ruled this city from 920 CE till the beginning of the thirteenth century.
6. The first animal sent to space.
7. Black Caps
8. Fort in Rajasthan constructed by Raja Man Singh I in 1592 and completed by Mirza Raja Jai Singh
9. It was the first Sanskrit work chosen for English translation by the Asiatic Society.
10. Caves discovered by an Army officer 107 km from Aurangabad
11. Reproduction of an organism or cell, or group of organisms or cells produced asexually from one ancestor or stock, to which they are genetically identical

12. A mammal of the giraffe family with dark chestnut coat and stripes on the hindquarters and front legs
13. Only city to be built on two continents
14. Spoor
15. Daughter of Vasant Khanolkar, leader of the Narmada Bachao Andolan
16. Malcolm Gray succeeded him as head of the ICC.
17. Mount Elbrus is located in this country.
18. This party was started by Netaji Subhas Chandra Bose in 1939.
19. This Indian athlete's autobiography is called *The Golden Girl.*
20. The Old Trafford stadium is the home of this football club.
21. Tourist attraction on river Sharavathi
22. Common to goddesses Lakshmi and Minerva
23. A trip or vacation taken by a newly-wed couple
24. This beverage is produced by steeping the leaves and leaf buds of the plant *Camellia sinensis* in boiling water.
25. Pongo, Perdita, Roger Radcliffe and Anita Radcliffe
26. It is always lit in Olympia, Greece, before the start of the Olympic Games.
27. A detective created by Carolyn Keene (a collective pseudonym used by Edward Stratemeyer and, among many others, his daughter Harriet S. Adams)
28. The first territorial possession of the Portuguese in Asia
29. The only prime minister of India to have signed a banknote.
30. Bangladesh borders this landlocked state on three sides.

31. The underwool of the endangered Tibetan antelope chiru
32. This Mughal emperor built the Shalimar Bagh for his wife.
33. The second largest continent after Asia in terms of area
34. Rajeshwar Prasad was this politician's real name.
35. The youngest Indian to complete the 1,000 runs and 100 wickets double feat in Test cricket.
36. This state was created out of the Bombay state along with Maharashtra.
37. He has a dog named Rocket and a truck named Dag-Dag.
38. Motilal Nehru's daughter, Jawaharlal Nehru's politician sister
39. The traditional Hindu science of medicine
40. This Indian has been called the 'Missing Nobel laureate'.
41. A middle eastern and Indian dish comprising of savoury balls made with minced meat, paneer or vegetables.
42. Moors and Tuaregs live in this desert.
43. William Sydney Porter
44. Reporter created by Hergé
45. Tourist attraction between lakes Erie and Ontario
46. The colours white, blue and red appear on the flag (horizontally, one after the other) from top to bottom
47. Overlooking a harbour, this structure in Australia looks like a sailboat.
48. This famous actress is Shomu Mukherjee's elder daughter.

49. This chemical element's symbol is Mn.
50. One of the wives of Shiva, daughter of the sage Daksha, later reborn as Parvati.

Answers on pages 158–160

VOCABULARY

1. Rearrange the word 'MADE' to get the feminine version of Sir.
2. Rearrange the word 'LOUSE' to get the name of a Korean city.
3. Rearrange the word 'MASTER' to get a flowing water body.
4. Rearrange the word 'CHAIN' to get the name of a country.
5. Rearrange the word 'MAUL' (as in being mauled or eaten by a tiger) to get the name of a white-ish mineral used to purify water or to stop bleeding of cuts.
6. Rearrange the word 'TABLE' to get the sound a sheep makes.
7. Rearrange the word 'DAWN' to get what magicians sometimes use.
8. Rearrange the word 'CLAM' to get a word meaning serene.
9. Rearrange the word 'SHORE' to get an animal.
10. Rearrange the word 'NOSE' to get the name of a river in Bihar.
11. Rearrange the word 'RAP' to get a golfing term.

12. Rearrange the word 'WHAT' to get a word to describe the melting of snow.
13. Rearrange the word 'SPICE' to describe books like the Ramayana and Mahabharata.
14. Rearrange the word 'PETAL' to find something on the dining table.
15. Rearrange the word 'RESIST' to get a member of your family.
16. Rearrange the word 'THROW' to get a word meaning value.
17. Rearrange the word 'ALSO' to find an Asia country.
18. Rearrange the word 'NEST' to get a kind of gun.
19. Rearrange the word 'POST' to put an end to motion.
20. Rearrange the word 'CARPEL' to get a word for goods wrapped up in a package.
21. Rearrange the word 'DUST' to find a place where horses are bred.
22. Rearrange the word 'GOAT' to get a Roman costume.
23. Rearrange the word 'CARE' to get a unit of land measurement.
24. Rearrange the word 'GAIN' to get a Hindu god.
25. Rearrange the word 'FALSE' to find the name of some insects.
26. Rearrange the word 'SINK' to get a body organ.
27. Rearrange the word 'LAST' to find a compound of sodium.
28. Rearrange the word 'TASTE' to find what Uttarakhand is.
29. Rearrange the word 'MARY' to find one of the wings of the armed forces.

30. Rearrange the word 'WENT' to find the name of an amphibian.
31. Rearrange the word 'DEAR' to get what you do when you open a book.
32. Rearrange the word 'PLANE' to get an Asian country.
33. Rearrange the word 'LEAK' to get a water body.
34. Rearrange the word 'LATE' to get a word that means story.
35. Rearrange the word 'SAVE' to get an object you might put flowers in.
36. Rearrange the word 'LEAST' to get a word that means 'to take something illegally or without permission'.
37. Rearrange the word 'NONE' to get a colourless gas.
38. Rearrange the word 'TIMER' to get a level of excellence.
39. Rearrange the word 'AGES' to get a religious person.
40. Rearrange the word 'HART' to get the name of a desert.
41. Rearrange the word 'SLIP' to get a part of your face.
42. Rearrange the word 'GNU' to get a name of a weapon.
43. Rearrange the word 'DONE' to get a part of a plant.
44. Rearrange the word 'LURE' to get a word that means king's reign.
45. Rearrange the word 'ERASE' to get an Indian garment.
46. Rearrange the word 'SALE' to get the name of a famous lioness.
47. Rearrange the word 'LUMP' to get a fruit.
48. Rearrange the word 'MORE' to get a city.

49. Rearrange the word 'MEAN' to get what people call you by.
50. Rearrange the word 'SLIDE' to get the name of a Hindi flim starring Shah Rukh Khan and Preity Zinta. (Hint: Two-word answer in Hindi.)

Answers on pages 160–161

VOCABULARY:
BACKWARDS OR FORWARDS

1. Read the word 'SMART' backwards to get a means of transport.
2. Read the word 'LAID' backwards to get what you do on the telephone.
3. Read the word 'BUS' backwards to get a prefix meaning lower.
4. Read the word 'NOW' backwards to get the basic monetary unit of North and South Korea.
5. Read the word 'KEEP' backwards to get a four-letter word meaning to take a brief look at something.
6. Read the word 'DEED' backwards to get a word that means 'an act or action'.
7. Read the word 'REWARD' backwards to find a compartment in your desk.
8. Read the word 'RATS' backwards to find a heavenly body.
9. Read the word 'GUM' backwards to get a drinking vessel.
10. Read the word 'TIDE' backwards to get a word that means to prepare for publication by correcting or modifying written material.

11. Read the word 'DESSERTS' (as in puddings) backwards, what word do you get?
12. Read the word 'YAM' backwards to get the name of a month.
13. Read the word 'STRAW' backwards to get a hard, rough growth on the surface of the skin.
14. Read the word 'EMIT' backwards to get a unit of measurement.
15. Read the word 'FLOW' backwards to get an animal's name.
16. Read the word 'ABLE' backwards to get where Napoleon was exiled.
17. Read the word 'SORE' to get the Greek god of love.
18. Read the word 'REPAID' backwards to get a baby's underpants.
19. Read the word 'FLOG' backwards to get the name of a game.
20. Read the word 'MADE' backwards to get a town in Holland or hard cheese.
21. Read the word 'LAGER' backwards to get a word meaning 'royal'.
22. Read the word 'BAT' backwards to get a computer key or small flap.
23. Read the word 'PART' backwards to get a device to catch animals.
24. Read the word 'LIAR' backwards to get what trains run on.
25. Read the word 'DRAW' backwards to get a room in a hospital.

Answers on pages 162

FUN FACTS 4

1. The oldest Nobel laureate in literature is Doris Lessing, who was eighty-eight years old when she was awarded the prize in 2007.
2. The five storeys of the Qutb Minar were built by different rulers of different dynasties. Qutb-ud-din Aibak constructed the base, his successor Iltutmish added the next three tiers and Firoz Shah Tughlaq added the fifth and last storey.
3. The flag of India is similar to the flag of Niger; the only difference being a small orange disc centred in the white band of the latter.
4. In the Harry Potter books, Albus Dumbledore has a scar above his knee which is shaped like the London Underground.
5. Six million hand-driven metal pins hold the Sydney Harbour Bridge together.
6. Yoshinori Sakai, a nineteen-year-old Japanese student, lit the Olympic flame at the Tokyo Games of 1964. He was chosen to light the flame because he was born near Hiroshima on 6 August 1945, the day the atomic bomb was dropped on the Japanese city.
7. No two gorilla noses are alike. Researchers in the wild

take close-up photographs of each gorilla's face to help identify individuals.

8. The Round Revolution ushered in an increase in the production of potatoes in India.

9. The word tsunami in Japanese literally translates to 'harbour wave'.

10. Yamuna is the other name of River Kalindi which turned black in colour when Shiva, after losing Sati, turned restless and plunged into it.

11. Tomato originated from the Andes. The first tomato was yellow, the size of a cherry, and named 'golden apple'. It was also called wolf's peach and Peruvian apple.

12. Geronimo was the code name of the operation to capture Osama Bin Laden. Incidentally, Geronimo was an Apache warrior who fought against the US and Mexico when they tried to invade parts of the native Indian lands.

SPOT THE ANSWER 3

1. Bidriware derives its name from the town of Bidar. In which state is Bidar located?
    a. Karnataka
    b. Kerala
    c. Gujarat

2. In which of these plants is the edible part called the 'tuber'?
    a. Potato
    b. Brinjal
    c. Onion

3. In literature, who met the Struldbrugs at Luggnagg?
    a. Robinson Crusoe
    b. Gulliver
    c. Sherlock Holmes

4. In India, who heads the Department of Space as a cabinet minister?
    a. The president
    b. The prime minister
    c. The defence minister

5. Among these countries, which was the first to defeat Australia in a Test match?
   a. South Africa
   b. Zimbabwe
   c. England

6. What does the Mohs scale measure?
   a. Density
   b. Velocity
   c. Hardness

7. The surname of which director of a hit film in 2005 was also the title of another popular film in the same year?
   a. *Mangal Pandey*
   b. *Sarkar*
   c. *Black*

8. What was defined as 'three grains of barley, dry and round, placed end to end lengthwise'?
   a. Centimetre
   b. Millimetre
   c. Inch

9. Which Indian dance form's earliest precursor is the Odhra Magadha?
   a. Kuchipudi
   b. Kathak
   c. Odissi

10. The name of which of these means the 'gilded one' in Spanish?

    a. El Dorado
    b. Buenos Aires
    c. El Nino

11. In the Mahabharata, who among these was killed by Krishna?
    a. Karna
    b. Ekalavya
    c. Jayadratha

12. Who was the last member of the Macedonian Ptolemaic dynasty to rule Egypt?
    a. Cleopatra
    b. Alexander
    c. Nero

13. Who was born in Gwalior in 1945 into the Bangash family as Masoom Ali Khan?
    a. Amjad Ali Khan
    b. Bismillah Khan
    c. Ali Akbar Khan

14. Which spice was first introduced to India around 1800 CE by the East India Company in its 'spice garden' in Courtallam, Tamil Nadu?
    a. Clove
    b. Pepper
    c. Cardamom

15. Abraham Ortelius's book, *Theatrum Orbis Terrarum,* which means 'Theatre of the World', is generally

believed to be the first modern example of which type of book?
a. Atlas
b. Dictionary
c. Encyclopedia

16. Which leader wrote the *Srimad Bhagavad Gita Rahasya* while he was jailed in Myanmar?
a. Bal Gangadhar Tilak
b. Motilal Nehru
c. Gopal Krishna Gokhale

17. Which of these tennis players is not of Belgian origin?
a. Mary Pierce
b. Kim Clijsters
c. Justin Henin-Hardenne

18. According to Thomas Alva Edison, what was 1 per cent inspiration and 99 per cent perspiration?
a. Genius
b. Happiness
c. His phonograph

19. 15 August 2005 marked the thirtieth anniversary of which pathbreaking film?
a. *Deewar*
b. *Mughal-e-Azam*
c. *Sholay*

20. On a standard computer keyboard, which of these keys has a left-pointing arrow on it?

    a. Backspace
    b. Enter
    c. Shift

21. Which famous historical city is situated on Sher Shah Suri Marg, 90 km from Delhi?
    a. Meerut
    b. Agra
    c. Panipat

22. In which of these states are you most likely to find the Chhotanagpur plateau?
    a. Andhra Pradesh
    b. Jharkhand
    c. Maharashtra

23. Which cricketer's autobiography is titled *Beyond Ten Thousand: My Life Story*?
    a. Imran Khan
    b. Allan Border
    c. Sunil Gavaskar

24. Which martyr used to write under the pseudonym Balwant Singh?
    a. Bhagat Singh
    b. Lala Lajpat Rai
    c. Chandrashekhar Azad

25. Which gemstone is commonly judged by the 'four Cs': carat, clarity, colour and cut?
    a. Opal

    b. Diamond

    c. Amethyst

26. On which musical instrument would you find 'siyahi'?
   a. Sitar
   b. Tabla
   c. Flute

27. Who was the first Indian to win the Ramon Magsaysay Award?
   a. Vinoba Bhave
   b. Jawaharlal Nehru
   c. S. Radhakrishnan

28. Which leader was also known as 'Frontier Gandhi'?
   a. Vallabhbhai Patel
   b. Abdul Ghaffar Khan
   c. Bal Gangadhar Tilak

29. Who was the first cricketer to score two centuries in his 100th Test match?
   a. Clive Lloyd
   b. Sachin Tendulkar
   c. Ricky Ponting

30. Which are the only cats to have a tuft or a bunch of hair at the end of their tail?
   a. Lions
   b. Tigers
   c. Jaguars

31. Which equation does David Bodanis call 'the world's most famous equation' in a biography of the equation?
    a. πr^2
    b. $E=mc^2$
    c. $D=sxt$

32. Which northeastern city in India derives its name from being the 'market for areca nut'?
    a. Guwahati
    b. Kohima
    c. Itanagar

33. Which of these musical instruments does not have any frets on its fingerboard?
    a. Violin
    b. Sitar
    c. Guitar

34. Which sea has often been called the incubator of Western civilization?
    a. Black Sea
    b. North Sea
    c. Mediterranean Sea

35. *Krrish* is the sequel to which Bollywood blockbuster?
    a. *Koi Mil Gaya*
    b. *Kabhi Khushi Kabhie Gham*
    c. *Mission Kashmir*

36. Which famous sultan of Delhi did Shihab-ud-din Umar succeed briefly in 1316?

   a. Ala-ud-din Khilji
   b. Muhammad bin Tughlaq
   c. Razia Sultana

37. With which art form is Anjolie Ela Menon associated?
   a. Literature
   b. Painting
   c. Music

38. Which mountain in Africa has three volcanic centres: Shira, Kibo and Mawenzi?
   a. Aconcagua
   b. Elbrus
   c. Kilimanjaro

39. *Tolkappiyam*, dated to around 500 BCE, is the earliest existing grammar of which Indian language?
   a. Marathi
   b. Gujarati
   c. Tamil

40. Which of these presidents of India was once the vice-chancellor of Aligarh University?
   a. Dr Zakir Hussain
   b. Dr Fakhruddin Ali Ahmed
   c. Dr A.P.J. Abdul Kalam

41. Whose wicket did Harbhajan Singh take to complete his Test hat-trick against Australia in 2000–01?
   a. Shane Warne
   b. Glenn McGrath
   c. Jason Gillespie

42. What does 'M' in MRI stand for?
    a. Musical
    b. Magnetic
    c. Mirror

43. Which film starring Aishwarya Rai is based on O. Henry's short story, 'The Gift of the Magi'?
    a. *Khaki*
    b. *Bride and Prejudice*
    c. *Raincoat*

44. The logo of which organization features a burning candle wrapped in barbed wire?
    a. Amnesty International
    b. Missionaries of Charity
    c. World Health Organization

45. Pichwais, large paintings on cloth, depict legends from the life of which god?
    a. Ganesha
    b. Krishna
    c. Kartikeya

46. In Sikkim, the name of which mountain means 'Five Treasures of the Great Snow'?
    a. Kanchenjunga
    b. Mount Everest
    c. Manaslu

47. In Hindu mythology, whose eighth son was named Devavrata?

a. Ganga
b. Ambika
c. Ambalika

48. Which Mughal emperor's last conquest was the fort of Asirgarh in the Deccan?
a. Shah Jahan
b. Jahangir
c. Akbar

49. As an offering to Krishna, every Brahmin or priest of the village of Kuchipudi is expected to perform which mythological character's role at least once in his life?
a. Radha
b. Rukmini
c. Satyabhama

50. Which city in Assam shares its name with one of the hottest chillies in the world?
a. Tezpur
b. Dibrugarh
c. Guwahati

Answers on pages 162–164

WHAT'S THE QUESTION 4

1. INRI meaning 'Jesus of Nazareth, King of the Jews'
2. An invigilator
3. Bhim and Maya are relatives of this Indian comic-strip character.
4. A druid
5. Big Ears and Mr Plod are his two friends.
6. A glass slipper helped the prince find her. (Hint: Fairy tales).
7. In *The Jungle Book*, Mother Wolf called him the 'frog'.
8. A lullaby
9. She was also known as Silver Hair, Silver Locks and Golden Hair.
10. Tongue-twister
11. The first woman president of India
12. In translation, it becomes 'Indian People's Party'.
13. It is a place where young children are cared for during the day while their parents work, study or shop.
14. It was the capital of British India from 1772 to 1912.
15. In computers, it is symbolized by a cup of steaming coffee.
16. Pedicab
17. Druk Yul, meaning 'Land of the Thunder Dragon'

18. Entire South and Central America including Mexico and parts of the Caribbean islands
19. Howie, AJ, Kevin, Brian and Nick form the group.
20. In Mumbai, this three-letter word for bread is often eaten with vada.
21. In Russia, he is called 'Grandfather Frost'.
22. It means 'thousand feet'.
23. She is known by her pet name Lolo.
24. Draco dormiens nunquam titillandus
25. He wrote *Aids to Scouting* and *Scouting for Boys.*
26. Jerry Siegel and Joe Shuster created this comic hero.
27. A ransom
28. The contestants in this sport wear a costume known as judogi.
29. A lasso
30. She was a Gorgon with snakes for hair.
31. A plagiarist
32. This spice is also called 'devil's dung'.
33. John Lennon, Paul McCartney, George Harrison and Ringo Starr
34. This era is said to have been started in 78 CE by Kanishka.
35. It comes from a Latin word meaning 'crawled'.
36. This precious stone is named after the Latin word for red.
37. This non-metallic brittle pale yellow solid has an atomic number 16.
38. Narendranath Dutta
39. She was the first woman to join the Indian Police Service in 1972.

40. His real name was Mahesh Das; his pen name was Brahma.
41. Pacemaker
42. The name of this comes from the Italian word meaning 'influence'.
43. He received the the United Nations Population Award in 1992.
44. Twenty-two yards in a cricket field
45. This North American city is built around Mount Royal.
46. He made his first public appearance in the comic strip 'Thimble Theatre' on 17 January 1929.
47. This Anglo-Indian term comes from the Portuguese for 'nurse'.
48. His sixtieth anniversary cartoons were called 'Popumentary'.
49. In the Chacha Chaudhary comics series, he is a friendly alien.
50. Aftershock (Hint: Geography)

Answers on pages 164–166

SPOT THE ANSWER 4

1. In literature, which author used the pseudonym Isaac Bickerstaff?
    a. Mark Twain
    b. Jonathan Swift
    c. Roald Dahl

2. Who was the British prime minister when India became independent?
    a. Clement Attlee
    b. Winston Churchill
    c. Harold McMillan

3. The name of which sport has been attributed to the French word meaning 'shepherd's crook'?
    a. Hockey
    b. Golf
    c. Polo

4. Which is the only member of the cat family that hunts primarily during the day?
    a. Cheetah
    b. Lion
    c. Tiger

5. For which film did Saif Ali Khan win the National Award for Best Actor?
   a. *Parineeta*
   b. *Hum Tum*
   c. *Kal Ho Naa Ho*

6. Archeological remains of which institution is found in the vicinity of a village called 'Bara Gaon' in the eastern part of India?
   a. Nalanda University
   b. Taxila University
   c. Ujjain Sun Temple

7. Which city in Uttarakhand would you go to if you want to attend the Kumbh Mela?
   a. Haridwar
   b. Dehra Dun
   c. Uttarkashi

8. In his travelogue, which island did Marco Polo refer to as the 'Female Island'?
   a. Minicoy
   b. Little Andaman
   c. Nicobar

9. According to Hindu mythology, who is the king of the yakshas?
   a. Kubera
   b. Skanda
   c. Yama

10. Which leader said, 'The blows, which fell on me today, are the last nails driven into the coffin of British imperialism'?
    a. Lal Bahadur Shastri
    b. Lala Lajpat Rai
    c. Bipin Chandra Pal

11. Which of these saris is traditionally from Gujarat?
    a. Patola
    b. Paithani
    c. Maheshwari

12. The name of which popular flavour comes from the Spanish word for 'pod'?
    a. Vanilla
    b. Strawberry
    c. Orange

13. In 2003, a newly discovered armoured dinosaur was named in honour of which famous science fiction author?
    a. Arthur C. Clarke
    b. Stephen King
    c. Michael Crichton

14. Who appoints the Attorney General of India?
    a. The president
    b. The prime minister
    c. The chief justice of the Supreme Court

15. Who was the first South African to score a double century on Test debut?

    a. Jacques Rudolph
    b. Andrew Hudson
    c. Kepler Wessels

16. What do a breed of penguins called Adelie penguins use to mark out their nests?
    a. Pebbles
    b. Fish
    c. Feathers

17. How many films starring Amitabh Bachchan start with the word 'Namak'?
    a. One
    b. Two
    c. Three

18. If '.in' is the Internet code of India, then '.zm' is the Internet code of which country?
    a. Zambia
    b. Zimbabwe
    c. South Africa

19. With which dance form would you associate the famous dancers Rukmini Devi Arundale and Yamini Krishnamurthy?
    a. Kathak
    b. Manipuri
    c. Bharatnatyam

20. Which island of New York has four counties: Kings, Queens, Nassau and Suffolk?

    a. Long Island
    b. Loyalty Islands
    c. Falkland Islands

21. Which deity rides the elephant Airavat?
    a. Indra
    b. Vishnu
    c. Shiva

22. Which Portuguese explorer became a page to Queen Leonor, wife of John II, in Lisbon at an early age?
    a. Ferdinand Magellan
    b. Christopher Columbus
    c. Marco Polo

23. Which Indian musician's father was the diwan of the Maharaja of Jhalawar?
    a. Pandit Ravi Shankar
    b. Ustad Zakir Hussain
    c. Pandit Shiv Kumar Sharma

24. What is the name of a Japanese dish consisting of small balls or rolls of vinegar-flavoured cold rice served with a garnish of vegetables, egg, or raw seafood?
    a. Falafel
    b. Tom yum
    c. Sushi

25. Which of these novels was written in verse?
    a. *The Glass Palace*

    b. *The God of Small Things*
    c. *The Golden Gate*

26. From 1977 to 1979, Atal Bihari Vajpayee was Union cabinet minister of...
    a. Information and Broadcasting
    b. External Affairs
    c. Civil Aviation

27. Kanyakubja was the former name of which ancient Indian city?
    a. Konark
    b. Kanauj
    c. Pataliputra

28. Hypocalcification, caused by insufficient calcium, results in the malformation of which part of the body?
    a. Teeth enamel
    b. Nail
    c. Hair

29. 'Time', one of M.F. Hussain's paintings, was inspired by the poem of which famous lyricist?
    a. Gulzar
    b. Javed Akhtar
    c. Sameer

30. If the colour of your school sweater is carmine, which colour is it?
    a. Deep red

b. Deep blue
c. Reddish-green

31. According to Acharya Vinoba Bhave 'Spirituality plus _____ = Sarvodaya'?
    a. Literature
    b. Science
    c. Politics

32. Lake Kawaguchi is noted for reflecting the image of which mountain in its waters?
    a. Mount Fuji
    b. Mount Kilimanjaro
    c. Mount Etna

33. In Hindu mythology, who received the title of Indrajit after he defeated Indra in a battle?
    a. Vibhishana
    b. Meghnad
    c. Kumbhakarna

34. In 643 CE, who summoned the Kanauj assembly to honour Hiuen Tsang?
    a. Harshavardhana
    b. Ashoka
    c. Kanishka

35. In a famous song from the film *Shree 420*, which accessory does Raj Kapoor describe as 'Roosi'?
    a. Patloon
    b. Topi
    c. Joota

36. In 1933, what name did Rabindranath Tagore choose for the baby born to the daughter of his secretary?
    a. Amartya
    b. Satyajit
    c. Kishore

37. Which prime minister of India was around three years old when India became independent?
    a. V.P. Singh
    b. Rajiv Gandhi
    c. I.K. Gujral

38. What is the name of 'five principles of peace' advocated by Pandit Nehru?
    a. Panchsheel
    b. Panch Yojna
    c. Panchavati

39. Which English cricketer as well as doctor was known for treating his poorer patients without charging a fee?
    a. Sir Donald Bradman
    b. Viv Richards
    c. W.G. Grace

40. Deodar is the national tree of which neighbouring country of India?
    a. Pakistan
    b. Bhutan
    c. Sri Lanka

41. The tagline of which of these films is 'It ain't the Cat in the Hat'?
    a. *Garfield*
    b. *Chicken Little*
    c. *Madagascar*

42. If a 'boomerang' is a throwing stick, what is a 'boomslang'?
    a. An African snake
    b. A bouncing ball
    c. A firecracker

43. What did Louis Braille lose while he was playing in his father's shop at the age of three?
    a. His teeth
    b. His sight
    c. His speech

44. Which river rises in the Black Forest mountains of western Germany and flows to the Black Sea?
    a. Danube
    b. Volga
    c. Rhine

45. In Hindu mythology, a black buffalo is the vahana/vehicle of which deity?
    a. Yama
    b. Indra
    c. Surya

46. The oldest capital of which south Indian dynasty was Uraiyur (now Tiruchirappalli)?
    a. Chola
    b. Pandya
    c. Chera

47. What was the name of Troy Bolton's basketball team in the film *High School Musical*?
    a. Wildcats
    b. Crazy Bears
    c. Black Panthers

48. Which of these vegetables forms the main ingredient of batata vada?
    a. Cauliflower
    b. Cabbage
    c. Potato

49. Which famous English author was born in 1903 in Motihari in Bihar?
    a. George Orwell
    b. Rudyard Kipling
    c. Ruskin Bond

50. What does Mysore Paints and Varnishes Limited provide during an election?
    a. Ballot box
    b. Indelible ink
    c. Electronic Voting Machine

Answers on pages 166–168

SPEED ROUND

In each set make a word using the first letters of the previous six answers. If the answer has more than one word, you can use the first letter of any of the words.

Set 1

1. Most of the world's rice are eaten by humans: serious or joking?
2. The name of which breed of dog comes from a German word meaning 'splash in water'?
3. Against which team did Brian Lara score 375 runs in a single Test innings: England or India?
4. Who wrote *The Praise of Folly*: Erasmus or Socrates?
5. Which element forms more compounds than all the other elements combined?
6. Of which small bird are giant, bee and ruby-throated species?
7. What is the word?

Set 2

1. Who is well known for his treatise on geometry called *The Elements*: Euclid or Plato?

2. In Hindu mythology, who was Nakula's mother: Madri or Draupadi?
3. The Louvre Museum is in which capital city: Paris or London?
4. If you have just landed at what was formerly known as Saddam Hussein International Airport, would you have landed in Iraq or Iran?
5. The three-letter name of which colour could be added after 'infra' to get the name of an electromagnetic radiation having wavelength less than microwaves?
6. What is the strong black coffee made by forcing steam through the ground coffee beans called?
7. What is the word?

Set 3
1. Who was the famous father of Amitabh Bachchan?
2. The name of which continent means 'opposite to the Arctic'?
3. Usually, what is the colour of metallic platinum: white or red?
4. Which NASA astronaut graduated from Tagore School, Karnal, India, in 1976?
5. Mammuthus is the extinct genus of which present-day animal?
6. On a tape deck, what is the opposite of a forward button?
7. What is the word?

Set 4
1. Who played Chandramukhi in Sanjay Leela Bhansali's *Devdas*: Aishwarya Rai or Madhuri Dixit?

2. Which team did Sri Lanka defeat to register its first-ever win in ODls: India or Zimbabwe?
3. What is the capital of Assam?
4. What comes after 'aloo' but before 'pukht': dum or kebab?
5. What does 'L' in LASER stand for?
6. Ocular albinism is a genetic condition that primarily affects which organ of the body?
7. What is the word?

Set 5

1. Who was the founder of the Mauryan dynasty: Chandragupta or Brihadratha?
2. Of which fruit are blood, navel and sour varieties: oranges or grapes?
3. In Hindu mythology, Swaha is the wife of which god: Agni or Indra?
4. Vasundhara Raje is a politician from which state: Maharashtra or Rajasthan?
5. Give me an eight-letter word starting with 'S' for 'something that serves as a reminder' of a place or event.
6. Which flightless bird is the second largest living bird?
7. What is the word?

Set 6

1. Most Indian alphabets have their origin in which script: Brahmi or Roman?
2. Kajol made her Hindi film debut with the 1992 film *Bekhudi*: agree or disagree?
3. What is the chemical symbol of potassium: P or K?

4. Which word announces the end of the first part in a cinema: interval or interchange?
5. Which is the most populous African nation?
6. Who was an Italian patriot: Guevara or Garibaldi?
7. What is the word?

Set 7

1. What does 'B' in VIBGYOR stand for: blue or brown?
2. Who saw forty thieves: Ali Baba or Aladdin?
3. Who was married to Raja Gangadhar Rao: Rani Padmini or Rani of Jhansi?
4. Who became chief minister earlier: Sheila Dikshit or Rabri Devi?
5. Which three letters are used as an abbreviation for 'et cetera'?
6. Who replaced Carl Hooper as the West Indian captain after the 2003 Cricket World Cup?
7. What is the word?

Set 8

1. What kind of animals are black panthers: leopards or lemurs?
2. Which part of the human body comes before brow, lash and lid?
3. What was USSR also known as: Soviet Union or Russia?
4. What kind of chips are used in computers: silicon or iron?
5. If 'Z' is the last letter in the English alphabet, then, what is the last letter in the Greek alphabet?

6. Against which team did Sachin Tendulkar score his only century at the 2003 Cricket World Cup?
7. What is the word?

Set 9

1. All trolleys have wheels: agree or disagree?
2. Who is also known as the Grand Old Man of India: Dadabhai Naoroji or Lala Lajpat Rai?
3. Which state has no coastline: Madhya Pradesh or West Bengal?
4. Who was a character in Shakespeare's *Othello*: Iago or Shylock?
5. What do politicians cut during most inauguration ceremonies?
6. In cricket, under which head are wides, no balls and byes classified?
7. What is the word?

Set 10

1. Copernicus is one of the most prominent craters on the moon: agree or disagree?
2. In *The Thousand and One Nights*, who recounts his adventures on seven voyages: Sindbad or Aladdin?
3. Which word describes a story or film containing events that precede those of an existing work: prequel or sequel?
4. The country Portugal is in which continent: Europe or Asia?
5. In a leap year, which festival is celebrated on the 360th day?

6. In a cricket match, what determines which team bats first?
7. What is the word?

Set 11
1. Which is a shade of purple: tan or mauve?
2. Which king adopted the policy of 'conquest by dharma': Samudragupta or Ashoka?
3. Black widow spiders are considered the most venomous spiders in North America: serious or joking?
4. In Greece, what is 'feta' a type of: cheese or butter?
5. Which term ending in 'bus', means a collection of work by an author, previously published separately?
6. Which set of seventy-eight cards, used for fortune telling, is divided into two groups called Major Arcana and Minor Arcana?
7. What is the word?

Set 12
1. With which sport is a 'dohyo' associated: sumo or judo?
2. Which of these is a snake-like fish: an eel or a seal?
3. Which ornament is worn around the neck: a bracelet or a choker?
4. In the official name of India, what comes before India: Republic or Union?
5. The River Volga flows through which continent?
6. Which Hindi film actress' sister is Farah?
7. What is the word?

Set 13

1. Which national park is situated 14 km from Sawai Madhopur and derives its name from the fort situated within its precincts?
2. In the country UAE, what does 'E' stand for: Empire or Emirates?
3. In Pakistan, what is a rupee divided into: paisa or cent?
4. Which Puri is a famous Indian actor: Aroon or Om?
5. 'The Night Watch' was one of which painter's most well-known paintings?
6. According to Western astrology, what is the zodiac sign of Sachin Tendulkar?
7. What is the word?

Set 14

1. Which Fidel is from Philippines: Ramos or Castro?
2. Harry Potter could talk to snakes: agree or disagree?
3. In which country would you find the Royal Chitwan National Park?
4. Which tone is emitted by a telephone: dial tone or earth tone?
5. What is the shape of the Oval Office, the official office of the president of the United States?
6. Which Dessau-born scholar was the son of the Romantic poet Wilhelm M¨uller?
7. What is the word?

Set 15

1. Which religious leader died at Kushinagar: Buddha or Mahavira?

2. What is the hard covering of the crown of teeth called: enamel or canine?
3. Who is related to Shabana Azmi: Kajol or Tabu?
4. What is the name of the cylindrical clay oven in which naans are made: tandoor or kadhai?
5. In which country is the Aswan High Dam located?
6. Which well-known musician's autobiography is *My Life, My Music*?
7. What is the word?

Set 16

1. Where does tartar accumulate: teeth or toes?
2. Who was older: Ashok Kumar or Kishore Kumar?
3. What is a religious teacher of the Jewish community called: a rabbi or a synagogue?
4. Who became the secretary of the Ahmedabad Textile Labour Association in 1992: Gulzarilal Nanda or Indira Gandhi?
5. What number batsman comes to bat after the sixth wicket falls?
6. Which state is famous for Tanjore paintings?
7. What is the word?

Set 17

1. Which country has a tricolour flag with white, blue and red bands: Canada or Russia?
2. What name is commonly given to the code of polite behaviour in society: epithet or etiquette?
3. Which surname is shared by the man who discovered Tutankhamun's tomb and the thirty-ninth US president: Carter or Clinton?

4. Biju Patnaik and his son Naveen Patnaik have been chief ministers of which Indian state?
5. In human blood, cells of which colour carry hemoglobin?
6. Commonly, which seven-letter name is given to a microcomputer suitable for use at an ordinary desk?
7. What is the word?

Set 18

1. Which of these is usually not encased in a shell: a walnut or a raisin?
2. What are most reptiles classified as: ectothermic or endothermic?
3. The Devnagari script uses forty-eight letters—thirty-four consonants and fourteen vowels and diphthongs: serious or joking?
4. In India what does 'I' in CBI stand for: investigation or intelligence?
5. Which five-letter word meaning 'magnificent' comes before Canyon and Slam?
6. Who is the famous mother of Sanjay Dutt?
7. What is the word?

Set 19

1. Which is the smallest member of the parrot family: pygmy or grey?
2. Which actress acted in Gurinder Chadha's *Bride and Prejudice*: Sushmita Sen or Aishwarya Rai?
3. Which fairy-tale character is famous for her long hair: Cinderella or Rapunzel?

4. In which Indian state is the annual Pushkar Fair held: Haryana or Rajasthan?
5. Which month gets its name from the Latin word for 'eight'?
6. Which cuddly toy gets its name from Theodore Roosevelt?
7. What is the word?

Set 20
1. What are bristol and bond two grades of: cheese or paper?
2. Grapes can also be black in colour: agree or disagree?
3. Which capital do Punjab and Haryana share: Srinagar or Chandigarh?
4. Which temperature scale is named after the British physicist William Thomson?
5. Which word is used to describe two objects or places at equal distances?
6. In computers, what is a program designed to breach security in the guise of performing some harmless function called?
7. What is the word?

SET 21
1. Which steel city lies along the Damodar river: Bokaro or Bilaspur?
2. Which of these is the heaviest living bird: ostrich or rhea?
3. Most skyscrapers are vertical or horizontal?
4. Which of these is a name for several Russian rulers: Ivan or Charles?

5. During which festival are snakes worshipped: Nag Panchami or Raksha Bandhan?
6. How many unit lengths will you use moving from minus 1 to 7?
7. What is the word?

SET 22

1. Which of these are more in number: countries or continents?
2. Which of these is the capital of Peru: Santiago or Lima?
3. What is a dome-shaped Eskimo house, typically built from blocks of solid snow, called?
4. Kim Jong-il was a leader of which country: South Korea or North Korea?
5. Give me a four-letter word for 'a soft, white substance formed when milk sours, used as the basis for cheese'.
6. Which of these parts of the human body serves as a pump: hair or heart?
7. What is the word?

Set 23

1. What are bowler and sombrero types of?
2. Which river is called Nahr al Furat in Arabic: Jordan or Euphrates?
3. In which city is the Lord's cricket ground: Manchester or London?
4. Which rock constitutes an estimated ninety-five per cent of the known crust of the Earth: igneous or sedimentary?

5. Which scheduled language of India is an official language of Pakistan?
6. According to the proverb, what does a rolling stone not gather?
7. What is the word?

SET 24

1. Ra is the chemical symbol of which element?
2. Which of these organizations has France and Belgium as its members: European Union or OPEC (Organization of Petroleum Exporting Countries)?
3. Ants can lift and carry more than three times their own weight: serious or joking?
4. Which Indian prime minister was born on 4 December 1919, in Jhelum?
5. In Hindu mythology, who was Lakshmana's father?
6. Which two-letter word comes before the painter 'Greco' and the climatic condition 'Nino'?
7. What is the word?

SET 25

1. In which language was the Ramayana composed: Hindi or Sanskrit?
2. Which district is in the state of Uttar Pradesh: Etah or Ernakulam?
3. Which nut is shaped like a bean: chestnut or cashew nut?
4. What is the Big Ben a type of: a tower clock or a cuckoo clock?
5. The scientific name of which bird is *Struthio camelus*?
6. Which flower is the symbol of the British Labour Party?

7. What is the word?

SET 26

1. Which comes earlier in a day: dusk or dawn?
2. Which of these teams has won a Football World Cup: Bolivia or Uruguay?
3. Catholics are Christians: serious or joking?
4. Where do the Wallace's flying frogs live almost exclusively: trees or mud?
5. Which continent starts with the letter 'E'?
6. With which everyday object would you associate King Gillette?
7. What is the word?

SET 27

1. What does 'D' in the title 'D.Litt' stand for: doctor or director?
2. Which of these has a milk base: yoghurt or shikanji?
3. Which is an amphibian: newt or electric eel?
4. Bats can fly: agree or disagree?
5. In the human body, striated, cardiac and smooth are all types of_____
6. Which epic by Homer deals with the wanderings of Odysseus after the fall of Troy?
7. What is the word?

SET 28

1. Which of these comes before the official name of Australia: Commonwealth or Republic?
2. Which of these cities is in Rajasthan: Udaipur or Ooty?

3. What lens would your grandfather use to correct his short sightedness: concave or convex?
4. Which niece of Rishi Kapoor made her debut opposite Abhishek Bachchan: Kareena Kapoor or Karishma Kapoor?
5. Which small word describes 'a pole with a blade used for rowing or steering a boat'?
6. Which is a citrus fruit: orange or banana?
7. What is the word?

SET 29

1. Ricky Ponting has scored the most number of Test centuries for Australia: agree or disagree?
2. Normally, in a pack of fifty-two playing cards, how many kings would you find?
3. What are Old Glory and Jolly Roger names of: flags or birds?
4. Quito is the capital of which country?
5. What is a rag doll made of?
6. In most cartoons, Indian politicians are shown wearing which type of topi?
7. What is the word?

SET 30

1. Which word describes 'a member of a sports team in their first full season': rookie or cookie?
2. Asmara is the capital of which country: Eritrea or Libya?
3. Which is the Maori word for 'peaks on the back': tarantula or tuatara?
4. Who look the same: fraternal twins or identical twins?

5. Which word derived from the Latin word for 'new' describes 'a star showing a sudden large increase of brightness'?
6. What do you call a person who has been tricked successfully on the first day of the fourth month?
7. What is the word?

SET 31

1. Florence Nightingale was born in Florence: agree or disagree?
2. Who among these has won both a Booker and a Nobel Prize: V.S. Naipaul or Salman Rushdie?
3. Which is the largest city in Australia?
4. Which national football team does Ryan Giggs represent: Wales or France?
5. Which ten-letter word, beginning with 'E', describes 'a person who has personally seen a thing happen and can give evidence'?
6. Which Indian president was the president of the Indian National Congress in 1934, 1939 and 1947?
7. What is the word?

SET 32

1. All the four states of south India have a coastline: agree or disagree?
2. In Hindi, which spice is known as 'saunf': fennel or fenugreek?
3. On which day do tableau presentations normally take place in front of VIPs in New Delhi: Republic Day or Independence Day?

4. Which word comes before hockey and skating: ice or water?
5. In navigation or surveying, which is the primary device to find a direction on Earth?
6. Which eleven-letter word starting with 'A' is a magician's favourite word?
7. What is the word?

SET 33
1. What did the Blue Mutiny refer to: indigo or rice?
2. Mount Cook is in New Zealand or Australia?
3. All planets are named after gods of Greek mythology: serious or joking?
4. Where is the archaeological site Sarnath located: Madhya Pradesh or Uttar Pradesh?
5. Which is the first fully air-conditioned train of india?
6. Which worm is also called angleworm?
7. What is the word?

SET 34
1. Spaniels are so called because they apparently originated in Spain: serious or joking?
2. In the abbreviation www, what does the third 'w' stand for: wide or web?
3. Which southeast Asian country declared its independence from the Netherlands on 17 August 1945?
4. Which spice is the dried, cleaned and polished rhizome of *Curcuma longa*: tamarind or turmeric?
5. Which famous leader was Rajmohan Gandhi's maternal grandfather?

6. The Greek word for sun, helios, was used in naming which element?
7. What is the word?

SET 35

1. As a prefix, 'sub' means under or over?
2. Which blood cells carry oxygen to body tissues: red blood cells or white blood cells?
3. Up to 2002, India had always beaten Pakistan at the Cricket World Cup: agree or disagree?
4. Who became the president of South Africa in 1994?
5. After Russia, which is the largest country in Europe in terms of area?
6. What word connects the following clues: a lucky number, dwarfs, wonders and continents?
7. What is the word?

SET 36

1. Which of these European nations is an island: Macedonia or Malta?
2. Which of these fruits is made into marmalade: oranges or mangoes?
3. Which scientist is more famous for his works on gravity: Newton or Herschel?
4. Which director would you associate with the films *Hero No. 1* and *Coolie No. 1*: David Dhawan or Mahesh Bhatt?
5. Who is the author of the book *Wings of Fire*?
6. Which part of the egg is also called deutoplasm?
7. What is the word?

SET 37

1. Which grow faster: fingernails or toenails?
2. Which boy's name is spoken in radio communication to convey that the message has been understood: Roger or Rover?
3. In which continent does the River Po flow: Africa or Europe?
4. Both the famous artists, Rembrandt and Vincent Van Gogh, belonged to the Netherlands or Italy?
5. What are autofocus and Polaroid two types of?
6. Which early Mughal ruler was also called Nasir-al-Din Muhammad?
7. What is the word?

SET 38

1. In *Gulliver's Travels*, what was Gulliver's first name: Lemuel or Samuel?
2. Hyder Ali was Tipu Sultan's father: agree or disagree?
3. Which of these is a marsupial: wombat or armadillo?
4. In Tintin comics, who was the Abominable Snowman?
5. Which cricket stadium is named after Lord Auckland's sisters: Eden Gardens or Green Park?
6. In which state is the Hawa Mahal located?
7. What is the word?

SET 39

1. In which of these films have Hema Malini and Amitabh Bachchan appeared together: *Baghban* or *Kal Ho Naa Ho*?
2. In dollar terms, which currency has a higher value: 1 Yen or 1 Euro?

3. Which commentator has not played Test cricket: Ravi Shastri or Harsha Bhogle?
4. Which state is larger in terms of area: Arunachal Pradesh or Manipur?
5. In Tibet, which breed of dog is called 'abso seng kye'?
6. How many angles does a pentagon have?
7. What is the word?

SET 40

1. Which fruit is commonly used as flavouring in golgappas: tamarind or mango?
2. Which Indian bowler made his Test debut in Australia: L. Balaji or Irfan Pathan?
3. What is the first name of the Indian painter M.F. Hussain: Mian or Maqbool?
4. The Ganges flows through Bihar or Tamil Nadu?
5. Which is the third planet from the sun and the fifth largest in our solar system?
6. Under Peter the Great, which country was proclaimed an empire in 1721: Italy or Russia?
7. What is the word?

Set 41

1. Which flower has a trumpet-shaped centre: dahlia or daffodil?
2. Which team has won more hockey gold medals in the Olympics: India or Pakistan?
3. Which epic means the 'great epic of the Bharata dynasty' in Sanskrit: the Ramayana or the Mahabharata?
4. Which city shares its name with a Trojan prince: Rome or Paris?

5. With which simple machine does the Hindi film comedian Johnny share his surname?
6. In which organ of the human body would you find the conjunctiva?
7. What's the word?

SET 42
1. What is a marmoset: a monkey or a parrot?
2. Sneezing is a reflex action of the human body: agree or disagree?
3. Which actress made a guest appearance in *Kal Ho Naa Ho*: Rani Mukherjee or Madhuri Dixit?
4. Majuli, one of the largest riverine islands in the world, is on which river?
5. In Hindu mythology, who was Sumitra's son: Lakshmana or Bharata?
6. Which 324 metre high European tower would you associate with Gustave Eiffel?
7. What is the word?

SET 43
1. Which country is landlocked: Mali or South Africa?
2. Adam Gilchrist has captained Australia in Test cricket: agree or disagree?
3. Which is a form of dance: twist or turn?
4. Who carried the first airmail in India: Tata or Birla?
5. Harpy, golden, bald and sea are different species of which bird?
6. Which four-letter name would you place before Pratap and after Jaspal?
7. What is the word?

SET 44

1. Which mythological character's name means 'Rama with an axe': Parashurama or Balaram?
2. After West Indies, which is the only team to win successive Cricket World Cups: Pakistan or Australia?
3. Who is the director of *Munnabhai MBBS*: Vidhu Vinod Chopra or Rajkumar Hirani?
4. Who was born in present-day Pakistan: Vajpayee or Advani?
5. Who is the spiritual head of the Tibetan Buddhists?
6. If you were facing north, which direction would your right hand point towards?
7. What is the word?

SET 45

1. Which moon would you find in the flag of Pakistan: crescent moon or full moon?
2. Armadillo is a Spanish word meaning 'little armoured one': agree or disagree?
3. In Maharashtra, which town is the site of Pandu and Chamar cave temples: Nasik or Ajanta?
4. Sirius, the brightest star in the night sky, is also called the Cat Star or Dog Star?
5. Give me a six-letter word for a traditional story popularly regarded as historical but not authenticated.
6. Till 1990, Germany was divided into West Germany and which other part?
7. What is the word?

SET 46

1. Gases that heat up the atmosphere by trapping sunlight

are called greenhouse gases or redhouse gases?

2. Which is awarded in more categories: the Oscars or the Nobel Prize?
3. In Scotland, what kind of a water body is a 'loch': a sea or a lake?
4. What was the name of a system of ethics founded by Akbar: Din-i-Ilahi or Baburnama?
5. Which actress is the sister of Ahana and the step sister of actor Bobby Deol?
6. Auckland is the largest urban area of which island nation?
7. What is the word?

Set 47

1. Anjolie Ela Menon is a famous actress or painter?
2. Another term used for a lift is an oscillator or an elevator?
3. Which of these is an Indian sweetmeat: rasmalai or rasam?
4. If P stands for Postal and N stands for Number, what does 'I' in PIN stand for: India or Index?
5. Which famous leader was born in Cuttack on 23 January 1897?
6. In which north Indian state would you be if you were sightseeing in Dalhousie?
7. What's the word?

SET 48

1. Who was the successor to Chandragupta I, the ruler of the Gupta empire?

2. Which state capital comes administratively under Papum Pare district: Itanagar or Kohima?
3. Rajapuri, langra and dussehri are some of the varieties of which fruit?
4. Which country has won the Cricket World Cup only once: West Indies or Pakistan?
5. According to Hindu myth, which flower is Jambudvipa, one of the seven continents, shaped like?
6. What is the currency of Cyprus?
7. What is the word?

SET 49
1. The sun is a star or a planet?
2. Which snake kills its victims using venom: the cobra or the python?
3. Sourav Ganguly is a left-handed or a right-handed bowler?
4. Amitabh Bachchan made his debut as an actor in *Saat Hindustani*: agree or disagree?
5. Which is Pakistan's most populous province?
6. Which eleven-letter word ending in 'ware' describes pots and dishes made of baked clay?
7. What is the word?

SET 50
1. Name Ralf Schumacher's brother who also competed in the same sport.
2. No two giraffes have the same pattern of spots: agree or disagree?
3. With which sport would you associate Franziska van Almsick?

4. Which of its world heritage sites does India share with Bangladesh: Sunderbans or Kaziranga National Park?
5. Who is the famous paternal grandmother of Rahul Gandhi?
6. F is the symbol of which chemical element?
7. What is the word?

Answers on pages 168–182

FACT PAGE 5

1. The National Sports of Canada Act, 1994, recognized ice hockey as its national winter sport and lacrosse as the national summer sport.
2. The words 'misplaced' and 'neighbouring', as well as the phrases 'green-eyed monster', 'out of work' and 'pound of flesh' were all coined by William Shakespeare.
3. Nawab Wajid Ali Shah, the Nawab of Avadh composed a number of songs and plays under the pen name Akhtari Pia.
4. One of Ganapati's tusks was broken by Parashurama in a duel when Ganapati stopped him from visiting a sleeping Shiva at Kailash.
5. The word 'coffee' comes from the Arab word qahwa, which translates as 'that which prevents sleep'.
6. The Buckingham Palace replaced St James's Palace as the official residence of the British monarch in 1698.
7. The sawfish is the only animal with true teeth outside its mouth.
8. The word 'mayday', used by vessels in an emergency, is derived from the French word 'm'aider', meaning 'help me'.

9. At the Olympics, India's medal tally for hockey includes eight golds, one silver and two bronzes.
10. Till over a century ago, it was thought that malaria was caused due to bad air.
11. In the 1770s, British explorer Captain Cook presented to the Tongan royal family a Madagascar radiated tortoise, which died in 1965, making the tortoise at least 188 years old.
12. In the Ramayana, when Rama fainted in a duel with Ravana, Kubera sent water purified by mantras to revive him.

ANSWERS

INDIA
1. Taj Mahal
2. Fa-hien
3. The Speaker
4. Lotus Temple
5. Also in Pokhran, Rajasthan
6. The Indian Penal Code
7. Tamil Nadu
8. Red Fort, New Delhi
9. Mother Teresa; she died on September 5
10. Holi
11. Gol Gumbaz
12. 'Chowk' means a town square or market and 'chowkidar' means a watchman.
13. Corbett National Park
14. 'Hookah' is a pipe and 'howdah' is the seat on an elephant.
15. Dadabhai Naoroji
16. Cattle fair
17. Shimla
18. 'Gopi' is a milkmaid and a 'gopuram' is a temple gateway.

19. Indira Gandhi
20. Karnataka
21. Madhya Pradesh
22. Florence Nightingale
23. Jamshedpur
24. Prince Khurram or Shah Jahan
25. Jharkhand
26. Cycle rickshaw
27. Border Security Force
28. Doddabetta, in theNilgiri mountain range
29. Gurmukhi
30. Ashokan Pillar Series
31. Kerala; the word derives from Calicut, now known as Kozhikode
32. Vallabhbhai Patel
33. Karnataka
34. Migraine
35. Viswanathan Anand
36. Mahabalipuram in Tamil Nadu
37. Krishnadevaraya
38. Lal Bahadur Shastri
39. Dog
40. Guwahati
41. Andhra Pradesh
42. Sunil Gavaskar
43. The Coast Guard
44. Siwalik Range
45. The Chipko Movement
46. 'Haveli' is a traditional mansion, 'havildar' is a soldier or police officer corresponding to a sergeant.
47. Atal Bihari Vajpayee

48. Ustad Allah Rakha Khan
49. Menaka
50. Great Indian Hornbill

SPORTS

1. Manchester United
2. Mushtaq Mohammad, 17 years and 78 days
3. Cricket
4. Prakash Padukone
5. Milkha Singh
6. Narain Karthikeyan
7. China
8. Rafael Nadal. In 2010, Rafael Nadal's US Open win over Novak Djokovic cemented the Spaniard's place in tennis history as one of only seven men to have won all four Grand Slam singles titles in their career.
9. Greece
10. Australia
11. Michael Schumacher
12. Table tennis
13. Koneru Humpy
14. Kamlesh Mehta
15. Mohinder Amarnath
16. Swati Ghate and S. Vijayalakshmi
17. Michael Johnson
18. Squash
19. Bangkok
20. St Moritz
21. Contract bridge
22. Madan Lal
23. Barcelona

24. Om Agarwal
25. Footballer for Germany
26. M.A.K. Pataudi
27. Ravi Shastri
28. Nandu Natekar
29. Magic Johnson
30. Dickie Bird
31. Syd is short for Sydney and Olly for Olympics
32. The All England Badminton Championships
33. Desmond Haynes
34. Thomas Lords
35. He holds up his flag above his head and waves it pointing to the player in offside position.
36. Dennis Amiss
37. Emmanuel Petit
38. Ice hockey
39. To protest against the Russian invasion of Afghanistan
40. Arthur Ashe
41. Life saving
42. Skydiving or free falling
43. Archery
44. You have to uproot one stump
45. Windsurfing
46. Don Bradman
47. Australia
48. Gymnastics
49. 10,000 metre
50. Baichung Bhutia

WHAT'S THE QUESTION 1
1.   What is an orangutan?

2. What are planetoids?
3. Who is Omar Abdullah?
4. What is tapioca?
5. Who was Samuel Morse?
6. Who is Baichung Bhutia?
7. What is a vada?
8. Who was Akela?
9. What is Rath Yatra?
10. What is a dragon?
11. When and where did the Boston Tea Party take place?
12. What does the word 'kremlin' mean?
13. Who was Akbar?
14. What does 'bonsai' mean?
15. What is a yak?
16. What is a frankfurter?
17. What is glucose?
18. Who is Noddy?
19. Name a district of Haryana.
20. What are the two types of camels?
21. What does the word 'Mahatma' mean?
22. What is Cotopaxi?
23. What is the NCC?
24. In computing, what is WORM?
25. What is New Zealand?
26. How is the 1919 Jallianwalla Bagh tragedy also known?
27. Name some endocrine glands in the human body.
28. Who is Lord Brahma?
29. Who was Raja Todar Mal?
30. Name the two official languages of Sri Lanka.
31. On the National Emblem, the elephant is the guardian of which direction?

32. What is per cent?
33. What does 'Mesopotamia' mean in Greek?
34. By what name was Bharatnatyam formerly known?
35. What is the Oval Office?
36. What is an elephant?
37. Name the two central characters in the Shakespearean play *The Taming of the Shrew*.
38. Who is Snoopy?
39. Who is Mickey Mouse?
40. What does RADAR stand for?
41. Who is Bholu?
42. What is the motto of the Olympic Games?
43. Where did Muhammad Bin Tughlaq shift his capital?
44. What was the tagline for *Jurassic Park*?
45. Which was the last book to feature Hercule Poirot?
46. What is the full form of ISKCON?
47. How do you complete a game of Ludo?
48. Who was Attila?
49. What was the former name of the capital of Tajikistan?
50. What is Hotmail?

SCIENCE
1. Kaziranga National Park
2. Rosettes
3. Gas
4. Blaise Pascal
5. The thyroid gland
6. Albert Einstein
7. Cactus
8. They were both deaf.
9. Ear

10. C.V. Raman
11. The good egg would sink.
12. Mars
13. From Armstrong, Aldrin and Collin, the three Apollo 11 astronauts
14. Louis Pasteur
15. Copper
16. Speed of light in vacuum
17. Inert gases or noble gases
18. Vinegar
19. Springbok
20. Hydrogen and oxygen
21. Brain
22. Rainbow
23. Thomas Alva Edison
24. Momentum
25. Knee
26. Subrahmanyan Chandrasekhar
27. Nosebleed
28. Eye
29. Basenji
30. Blood pressure
31. Alternate
32. *Swades*
33. Brinjal
34. 2
35. Octopus
36. Iodine
37. Vitamin C
38. Femur/thighbone
39. Bile

40. Water
41. Meghnad Saha
42. Carbon copy
43. Calcium
44. Vaccination
45. Teeth. It is the dental formula.
46. Australia
47. Hydrogen
48. Lungs
49. William Shakespeare
50. Three

LANGUAGE AND LITERATURE

1. The second hand
2. Kalidasa
3. You wear a perfume.
4. *Natyashastra*
5. Types of poems
6. Atal Bihari Vajpayee
7. Panchatantra
8. David Copperfield
9. Ruskin Bond
10. Goat
11. Buddhism
12. Taurus
13. Premchand
14. Explode means to burst outwards and implode means to collapse inwards
15. Sheep
16. *Twenty Thousand Leagues Under the Sea*
17. Alpha and beta

18. *Hamlet*
19. Mulk Raj Anand
20. Iron
21. Charles Dickens
22. *Moby Dick*
23. Huckleberry Finn
24. Scrooge
25. *Uncle Tom's Cabin*
26. *Pride and Prejudice*
27. Bank
28. Bill and Hillary Clinton
29. Stephen Hawking
30. *The Wonderful Wizard of Oz*
31. Arundhati Roy
32. A person whose job it is to write material for someone else who is a named author.
33. Albino
34. Colon
35. The Count of Monte Cristo
36. Christmas
37. Poach
38. Jim Corbett
39. Chinese
40. Chaitanya
41. Leo Tolstoy
42. Amrita Pritam
43. Hogwarts
44. Bhishma
45. Mark Twain
46. Macbeth
47. Pickpocket

48. Amrita Pritam
49. Winnie the Pooh
50. *Uncle Tom's Cabin*

SPOT THE ANSWER 1

1. a. Rs 10
2. c. Taxila
3. b. Shiva
4. c. Gestapo
5. b. Andhra Pradesh
6. b. Raja Ravi Varma
7. c. Mississippi
8. a. The vice president
9. c. Aikido
10. b. Wild ass
11. b. Shoe
12. a. Maulana Abul Kalam Azad
13. a. Salt. When applied to snow or ice, salt lowers the melting point of the mixture.
14. b. Strong underwater earthquakes
15. a. Parashurama
16. a. Mahatma Gandhi
17. a. Sitar
18. a. Bread pieces
19. b. Old Dame Dob
20. b. Uttar Pradesh
21. b. Brian Lara
22. b. Chlorine
23. b. Rahul Bose
24. b. July
25. a. Hindi and English

26. d.   Aravalli
27. a.   Ass
28. a.   Khajuraho. It is a village in Madhya Pradesh.
29. c.   Odissi
30. c.   Saffron
31. a.   Patil
32. a.   Attorney General
33. c.   Dickie Bird
34. b.   Antarctica
35. a.   *Black*
36. a.   Machine (ATM = Automated Teller Machine)
37. c.   Phulkari
38. c.   Chandigarh
39. a.   Ramayana
40. c.   Lewis Carroll
41. c.   Bharata Muni
42. a.   Momo
43. a.   R.L. Stevenson
44. b.   Sarojini Naidu
45. c.   West Indies
46. b.   Woodpeckers
47. a.   Jawaharlal Nehru
48. a.   Mridangam
49. a.   The Constitution of India
50. a.   Persian Gulf

MYTHOLOGY
1.   Ravana
2.   Ganesha
3.   Sita
4.   Shiva

5. Gandhari
6. Krishna
7. Dhanwantari
8. Takshak
9. Purochana
10. Balabhadra (Balarama, Baladeva)
11. His heel
12. Durga
13. Bhima
14. Dronacharya. He got his name from 'drona' meaning bucket.
15. Shiva
16. Valmiki
17. Vishwakarma
18. Thor
19. Indrajit
20. Gorgons
21. Pan
22. Jaya
23. Heracles. He was the son of Zeus and Alcmene.
24. Ved Vyasa
25. Olympus
26. Uttara's dance and music teacher
27. Balarama
28. The jackal
29. Vishwakarma. He is the architect of the gods.
30. He was the dairyman.
31. Frigg
32. Indra
33. Mnemosyne
34. Mareecha

35. Vibhishana
36. King Arthur
37. Vishwakarma
38. Arjuna
39. Ravana
40. Lord Vishnu
41. Mars
42. Shatrughna
43. Dhrishtadyumna. He was Draupadi's brother.
44. Saraswati
45. Narada
46. Sahadeva
47. Echo
48. Satyavati
49. Pandora
50. Sudarshan

MIXED BAG 1

1. *Alice's Adventures in Wonderland*
2. Pandit Birju Maharaj; Kalashram is in New Delhi
3. The Indian National Flag
4. Dalmatian
5. Indian currency notes
6. Mica
7. Neptune
8. Arunachal Pradesh. Many tribes such as the Nyishis, Hill Miris, Akas, Buguns and Mijis depend on the Apatanis for their supply of cloth.
9. Politics
10. Parliament of India
11. Shaktimaan

12. Chikankari
13. Public service
14. Santoor
15. Menthol
16. Rajendra Prasad
17. Iris
18. England and West Indies
19. Bada Imambara
20. Penicillin
21. Children's literature
22. Embedded
23. Germany
24. Eighteen
25. Question Hour
26. Puppetry
27. Mahatma Gandhi at Sabarmati
28. Varanasi's sacred bathing ghats
29. Florence Nightingale
30. The Kushanas
31. Alfred Bernhard Nobel
32. S.H.F.J. Manekshaw
33. Meghalaya
34. Mauritius
35. Emerald
36. Swastika
37. *Gulliver's Travels*
38. Pandit Hariprasad Chaurasia
39. Pygmy
40. East Timor
41. Hippopotamus
42. Five

43. Michael Vaughan
44. The Iron Pillar of Mehrauli
45. Dandruff
46. Lightning
47. No man's land
48. E.M.S. Namboodiripad
49. South Pole
50. Pondicherry

WHAT'S THE QUESTION 2

1. Who was Kaikeyi?
2. What is a lagoon?
3. Who was Helen Keller?
4. Where do the Powerpuff Girls stay?
5. Who is a knight?
6. What is a sauna?
7. Who was Mohammad Ali Jinnah?
8. What is a tola?
9. What is penicillin?
10. Who is Harry Potter?
11. What is a flowchart?
12. Who was Jesse Owens?
13. What is Rakhi or Raksha Bandhan?
14. What is the meaning of the word 'ski'?
15. What is skin?
16. Who was Helen of Troy?
17. What is tea?
18. What is Chilka Lake?
19. Who are the Spice Girls?
20. What does the word 'architect' mean?
21. What is a dashboard?

22. What are daffodils?
23. What are momos?
24. Who was the Duke of Wellington?
25. What is the India Gate also known as?
26. What is sublimation?
27. What is the caribou?
28. What is khaki?
29. In what way was President Zakir Husain a first?
30. Who is Sunil Gavaskar?
31. Who was Uncle Tom?
32. Winston Churchill
33. Name Harry Potter's pet.
34. What is Pekingese?
35. What is friction?
36. Who is V.V.S. Laxman?
37. Who was Harry S. Truman?
38. What is the name of the airport that serves Hyderabad?
39. Who was Agatha Christie?
40. What was the Gestapo?
41. Who is Desmond Tutu?
42. What is Mercury?
43. What is relativity?
44. What is vanilla?
45. Name the Indian twin characters created by J.K. Rowling.
46. Why was the Charminar built?
47. Who is Snoopy?
48. Who was Donald Bradman?
49. Which is the largest satellite of Neptune?
50. What is the Rigveda?

GEOGRAPHY

1. Egypt
2. Red
3. Dragon
4. Brahmaputra
5. Mount Everest
6. Tripura
7. The Sydney Harbour Bridge. It is known as the 'coathanger' because of its arched shape.
8. India
9. Alaska
10. Antarctica
11. Denmark
12. Nitrogen
13. Gangtok
14. Jigsaw puzzles
15. Laos
16. West Bengal
17. Texas
18. Kenya and Libya
19. Yemen
20. Simpson
21. Jammu
22. K2
23. Qatar
24. Gibraltar
25. Sri Lanka
26. Turkey
27. Andhra Pradesh and Arunachal Pradesh
28. Indonesia
29. Sabarmati

30. Haflong
31. Jodhpur
32. Khajuraho
33. Goa
34. Orissa
35. Haryana
36. Rana Kumbha
37. Jahangir
38. Rats
39. Auroville
40. Meghalaya
41. Alappuzha
42. Himachal Pradesh
43. Germany
44. Devil's Tower
45. Ayers Rock
46. Kanchenjunga
47. Turkey
48. Chennai
49. The Rock Garden
50. K2

ENTERTAINMENT

1. Superman
2. Sunil Gavaskar
3. Shahid Kapoor
4. They are all boy bands.
5. *Shrek*
6. Records (LPs)
7. Mickey Mouse
8. Tweety Pie

9. Anchors as well
10. Amitabh Bachchan
11. Ustad Nusrat Fateh Ali Khan
12. *Sholay*
13. Alisha Chinai
14. Tom and Jerry (Initially named Jasper and Jinx, only Tom was identified as Jasper onscreen.)
15. Delhi
16. Getafix
17. William Tell
18. Tarzan
19. B*Witched
20. Velma
21. *The Calculus Affair*
22. Ricky Martin
23. Cacofonix
24. Dwayne 'The Rock' Johnson
25. Scrabble
26. Sanjay Dutt
27. *Asterix the Gaul*
28. Spider-Man
29. Butcher
30. Urmila Matondkar
31. The SWAT Kats
32. Hrithik Roshan
33. Rabbi Shergill
34. *Sarkar*
35. Strings
36. Kishore Kumar
37. Anthony Gonsalves

38. Sarod (Ustad Amjad Ali Khan)
39. Sanskrit
40. M.F. Hussain
41. Kajol
42. *The Pianist*
43. Anand Milind
44. Anoushka Shankar
45. Odissi
46. Satyajit Ray
47. Rabindranath Tagore
48. Hands and lips
49. Harp
50. Apron

SPOT THE ANSWER 2

1. b. Treta yuga
2. c. Third. Ahmad Shah Abdali defeated the Marathas in 1761.
3. c. Krishna
4. a. Shrikhand, indigenous to Maharashtra and Gujarat
5. b. Dalai Lama
6. b. One-third
7. c. Sunil Gavaskar
8. c. Tiger
9. a. Munshi Premchand
10. c. Rabab
11. c. Asian Games inauguration
12. a. Andaman and Nicobar Islands
13. c. Shanta
14. a. Liver
15. b. Wax

16. c.   Pasta
17. c.   *Raghuvansham*
18. a.   Ganesha
19. a.   Billiards
20. b.   Deer
21. a.   Dog
22. b.   M.F. Hussain
23. c.   Blue pottery
24. b.   Mizoram
25. c.   Sita
26. a.   Platinum
27. c.   Haryana
28. b.   Cashew nut
29. b.   Taj Mahal
30. b.   Sri Lanka
31. a.   FIFA World Cup 2002
32. a.   Sperm whale
33. a.   Nagesh Kukunoor
34. b.   E
35. a.   Economy
36. a.   Marie Curie
37. b.   Kanva
38. c.   Clove
39. a.   Sarod
40. a.   Coriander
41. a.   Leo Tolstoy
42. a.   Charan Singh
43. b.   Agra
44. b.   Moon
45. c.   Shah Rukh Khan
46. b.   Computer. It is a small ball that is set in a holder

and can be rotated by hand to move a cursor on a computer screen.
47. b. First film screening
48. b. Turkey (Greater Ararat)
49. a. Abhimanyu
50. a. Buddha's feet or footprints

MIXED BAG 2

1. Yet; Yet Another Hierarchical Officious Oracle
2. Football
3. Pasteurization
4. Red
5. Dog
6. Bangladesh
7. Turkey
8. Tennis
9. Bird
10. Spain
11. Escape
12. Football
13. Monica Seles
14. Subrahmanyan Chandrasekhar
15. Assam
16. Computer Aided Design
17. Andes
18. Tennis
19. Tamil Nadu
20. South America
21. Fifteen
22. C.V. Raman
23. Boxing

24. Ellora Caves
25. Anne Boleyn
26. Olive
27. Rajasthan
28. Bangladesh
29. Archery
30. Gateway of India
31. Tamil Nadu
32. Cricket
33. Palace on Wheels
34. Silk
35. Gnu
36. Beginner's; Beginner's All-purpose Symbolic Instruction Code
37. Equestrian
38. Ludo
39. Barkhan or barchan
40. Fork
41. Site
42. Puma
43. Theodore Roosevelt
44. Gross
45. Tennis
46. Pixel
47. Melbourne
48. Lal Bahadur Shastri
49. R.K. Narayan
50. Auguste Rodin

HISTORY
1. Rajasthan

2. Sita
3. Victory
4. All were assassinated.
5. Swami Vivekananda
6. Padmaja Naidu
7. *Pravda*
8. Germany
9. S. Radhakrishnan
10. Isabel Perón
11. Harishchandra
12. West Bengal
13. Humayun
14. Khan Abdul Ghaffar Khan
15. The Bahmani kingdom
16. C. Rajagopalachari
17. Egypt
18. Buddhist Councils
19. Black Death
20. Tartars
21. Sir Winston Churchill
22. Queen Elizabeth
23. World War I
24. Adolf Hitler
25. Neil Armstrong and Edwin Aldrin
26. Omar Mukhtar
27. Genghis Khan
28. Michelangelo
29. Bahadur Shah II
30. Marriage/Matrimonial alliance
31. Red Fort
32. Winston Churchill

33. Khadi
34. Oslo
35. Jesus's cup from the Last Supper
36. Karl Marx
37. Florence Nightingale
38. Humayun
39. Pratihara
40. Mahatma Gandhi
41. George Yule
42. Mother Teresa
43. Ala-ud-din Khilji
44. Mahatma Gandhi
45. Mahatma Gandhi
46. French Revolution
47. Sher Shah Suri
48. Akbar
49. Buddha
50. Nadir Shah

WHAT'S THE QUESTION 3

1. Who is Big Ears?
2. What is Ujjain famous for hosting?
3. What does the flag of Brazil feature?
4. Who was Queen Victoria?
5. What is Madurai?
6. Who was Laika?
7. What is the nickname of the New Zealand cricket team?
8. What is Amber?
9. What is the Ramayana?
10. Where are the Ajanta Caves?
11. What is cloning?

12. What are okapis?
13. What is Istanbul?
14. What is the track or scent of an animal?
15. Who is Medha Patkar?
16. Who succeeded Jagmohan Dalmiya?
17. What is Russia?
18. What is the Forward Bloc?
19. What is the name of P.T. Usha's autobiography?
20. Which is the home ground of Manchester United?
21. What are the Jog Falls?
22. Which two goddesses are connected by an owl?
23. What is a honeymoon?
24. What is tea?
25. Name some characters from the 1961 film *101 Dalmatians*.
26. Where is the Olympic flame always lit before the start of the Olympics?
27. Who is Nancy Drew?
28. What is Goa?
29. Who is Manmohan Singh?
30. What is Tripura?
31. What is shahtoosh?
32. What did Jahangir build for Nur Jahan in Srinagar?
33. What is Africa?
34. What was Rajesh Pilot's real name?
35. Who is Kapil Dev?
36. What is Gujarat?
37. Who is Chacha Chaudhary?
38. Who was Vijaya Lakshmi Pandit?
39. What is Ayurveda?
40. Who was Mahatma Gandhi?

41. What are koftas?
42. What are the tribes of the Sahara?
43. What was O. Henry's original name?
44. Who is Tintin?
45. What are the Niagara Falls?
46. Describe the flag of Russia.
47. What is the Sydney Opera House?
48. Who is Kajol?
49. What is manganese?
50. Who is Sati?

VOCABULARY
1. DAME
2. SEOUL
3. STREAM
4. CHINA
5. ALUM
6. BLEAT
7. WAND
8. CALM
9. HORSE
10. SONE
11. PAR
12. THAW
13. EPICS
14. PLATE
15. SISTER
16. WORTH
17. LAOS
18. STEN
19. STOP

20. PARCEL
21. STUD
22. TOGA
23. ACRE
24. AGNI
25. FLEAS
26. SKIN
27. SALT
28. STATE
29. ARMY
30. NEWT
31. READ
32. NEPAL
33. LAKE
34. TALE
35. VASE
36. STEAL
37. NEON
38. MERIT
39. SAGE
40. THAR
41. LIPS
42. GUN
43. NODE
44. RULE
45. SAREE
46. ELSA
47. PLUM
48. ROME
49. NAME
50. DIL SE

VOCABULARY: BACKWARDS OR FORWARDS

1. TRAMS
2. DIAL
3. SUB
4. WON
5. PEEK
6. DEED
7. DRAWER
8. STAR
9. MUG
10. EDIT
11. STRESSED
12. MAY
13. WARTS
14. TIME
15. WOLF
16. ELBA
17. EROS
18. DIAPER
19. GOLF
20. EDAM
21. REGAL
22. TAB
23. TRAP
24. RAIL
25. WARD

SPOT THE ANSWER 3

1. a. Karnataka
2. a. Potato
3. b. Gulliver

4. b. The prime minister
5. c. England
6. c. Hardness
7. b. *Sarkar*. *Sarkar* and Pradip Sarkar, director of *Parineeta*.
8. c. Inch
9. c. Odissi
10. a. El Dorado
11. b. Ekalavya
12. a. Cleopatra
13. a. Amjad Ali Khan
14. a. Clove
15. a. Atlas
16. a. Bal Gangadhar Tilak
17. a. Mary Pierce
18. a. Genius
19. c. *Sholay*. It was released on 15 August 1975.
20. b. Enter
21. c. Panipat. Sher Shah Suri Marg is part of National Highway 1.
22. b. Jharkhand
23. b. Allan Border
24. a. Bhagat Singh
25. b. Diamond
26. b. Tabla. Siyahi are the black spots on the tabla.
27. a. Vinoba Bhave
28. b. Abdul Ghaffar Khan
29. c. Ricky Ponting
30. a. Lions
31. b. $E=mc^2$
32. a. Guwahati

33. a. Violin
34. c. Mediterranean Sea
35. a. *Koi Mil Gaya*
36. a. Ala-ud-din Khilji
37. b. Painting
38. c. Kilimanjaro
39. c. Tamil
40. a. Dr Zakir Hussain
41. a. Shane Warne
42. b. Magnetic
43. c. *Raincoat*
44. a. Amnesty International
45. b. Krishna
46. a. Kanchenjunga
47. a. Ganga
48. c. Akbar
49. c. Satyabhama
50. a. Tezpur

WHAT'S THE QUESTION 4

1. What is inscribed on Jesus's cross?
2. What would you call a person who supervises candidates at an examination?
3. Who is Pavitra Prabhakar?
4. What would you call an ancient Celtic priest, magician or soothsayer?
5. Name two of Noddy's friends.
6. Who was Cinderella?
7. Who was Mowgli?
8. What do you call a quiet, gentle song sung to send a child to sleep?

9. What was Goldilocks also known as?

10. What do you call a sequence of words difficult to pronounce quickly and correctly?

11. Who is Pratibha Patil?

12. What does Bharatiya Janata Party mean?

13. What is a créche?

14. What important position did Calcutta hold under the British?

15. How is Java, the computer language, usually symbolized?

16. What is a small pedal-operated vehicle, serving as a taxi in some countries?

17. What do the locals call Bhutan?

18. Which countries make up Latin America?

19. Who are the members of the group the Backstreet Boys?

20. What is a 'pav'?

21. How is Santa Claus known in Russia?

22. What does the word 'millipede' mean?

23. What is Karishma Kapoor's nickname?

24. What is the motto of Hogwarts School of Witchcraft and Wizardry?

25. Name two well-known books by Lord Baden-Powell.

26. Who were the creators of Superman?

27. What do you call a sum of money paid for the release of a hostage or a prisoner?

28. What is Judo?

29. What do you call a rope with a noose at the end used for catching cattle?

30. In Greek mythology, who was Medusa?

31. What do you call someone who copies a literary work or invention and passes it off as his own?

32. What is asafoetida?
33. Who are the musicians who make up the band the Beatles?
34. Which Indian ruler started the Saka era?
35. What is the origin of the word 'reptiles'?
36. What is ruby?
37. What is sulphur?
38. What was Swami Vivekananda's real name?
39. Who is Kiran Bedi?
40. Who was Birbal?
41. Which device is used for stimulating the heart muscle?
42. What is influenza/flu?
43. Who was J.R.D. Tata?
44. What is the length of a cricket pitch?
45. How did Montreal get its name?
46. Who is Popeye?
47. What does the word 'ayah' mean?
48. What were the series of six prime-time special cartoons on Popeye's sixtieth anniversary called?
49. Who is Sabu?
50. What do you call a tremor or series of tremors that occur after an earthquake?

SPOT THE ANSWER 4

1. b. Jonathan Swift
2. a. Clement Attlee
3. a. Hockey
4. a. Cheetah
5. b. *Hum Tum*
6. a. Nalanda University
7. a. Haridwar

8. a. Minicoy
9. a. Kubera
10. b. Lala Lajpat Rai
11. a. Patola
12. a. Vanilla (The flavouring essence is derived from the pods of the vanilla orchid.)
13. c. Michael Crichton
14. a. The president
15. a. Jacques Rudolph
16. a. Pebbles
17. b. Two. The two films are *Namak Haram* and *Namak Halal*.
18. a. Zambia
19. c. Bharatnatyam
20. a. Long Island
21. a. Indra
22. a. Ferdinand Magellan
23. a. Pandit Ravi Shankar
24. c. Sushi
25. c. *The Golden Gate*
26. b. External Affairs
27. b. Kanauj
28. a. Teeth enamel
29. b. Javed Akhtar
30. a. Deep red
31. b. Science
32. a. Mount Fuji
33. b. Meghnad
34. a. Harshavardhana
35. b. Topi. The song was sung by Mukesh.
36. a. Amartya

37. b.   Rajiv Gandhi
38. a.   Panchsheel
39. c.   W.G. Grace
40. a.   Pakistan
41. a.   *Garfield*
42. a.   An African snake
43. b.   His sight
44. a.   Danube
45. a.   Yama
46. a.   Chola
47. a.   Wildcats
48. c.   Potato
49. a.   George Orwell
50. b.   Indelible ink

SPEED ROUND

Set 1
1. Serious
2. Poodle
3. England
4. Erasmus
5. Carbon
6. Hummingbird
7. SPEECH

Set 2
1. Euclid
2. Madri
3. Paris
4. Iraq

5. Red
6. Espresso
7. EMPIRE

Set 3
1. Harivansh Rai Bachchan
2. Antarctica
3. White
4. Kalpana Chawla
5. Elephant
6. Rewind button
7. HAWKER

Set 4
1. Madhuri Dixit
2. India
3. Dispur
4. Dum
5. Light
6. Eyes
7. MIDDLE

Set 5
1. Chandragupta Maurya
2. Oranges
3. Agni
4. Rajasthan
5. Souvenir
6. Emu
7. COARSE

Set 6
1. Brahmi
2. Agree
3. K
4. Interval
5. Nigeria
6. Garibaldi
7. BAKING

Set 7
1. Blue
2. Ali Baba
3. Rani of Jhansi
4. Rabri Devi
5. Etc.
6. Brian Lara
7. BARREL

Set 8
1. Leopards
2. Eye
3. Soviet Union
4. Silicon
5. Omega
6. Namibia
7. LESSON

Set 9
1. Agree
2. Dadabhai Naoroji
3. Madhya Pradesh

4. Iago
5. Ribbon
6. Extras
7. ADMIRE

Set 10
1. Agree
2. Sindbad
3. Prequel
4. Europe
5. Christmas
6. Toss
7. ASPECT

Set 11
1. Mauve
2. Ashoka
3. Serious
4. Cheese
5. Omnibus
6. Tarot cards
7. MASCOT

Set 12
1. Sumo
2. Eel
3. Choker
4. Republic
5. Europe
6. Tabu
7. SECRET

Set 13
1. Ranthambore National Park
2. Emirates
3. Paisa
4. Om
5. Rembrandt
6. Taurus
7. REPORT

Set 14
1. Ramos
2. Agree
3. Nepal
4. Dial tone
5. Oval
6. Max Müller
7. RANDOM

Set 15
1. Buddha
2. Enamel
3. Tabu
4. Tandoor
5. Egypt
6. Pandit Ravi Shankar
7. BETTER

Set 16
1. Teeth
2. Ashok Kumar
3. Rabbi

4. Gulzari Lal Nanda
5. Eight
6. Tamil Nadu
7. TARGET

Set 17

1. Russia
2. Etiquette
3. Carter; Howard Carter and Jimmy Carter
4. Orissa
5. Red
6. Desktop
7. RECORD

Set 18

1. Raisin
2. Ectothermic
3. Serious
4. Investigation
5. Grand
6. Nargis
7. RESIGN

Set 19

1. Pygmy
2. Aishwarya Rai
3. Rapunzel
4. Rajasthan
5. October
6. Teddy bear
7. PARROT

Set 20
1. Paper
2. Agree
3. Chandigarh
4. Kelvin Scale
5. Equidistant
6. Trojan Horse
7. PACKET

Set 21
1. Bokaro
2. Ostrich
3. Vertical
4. Ivan
5. Nag Panchami
6. Eight
7. BOVINE

Set 22
1. Countries
2. Lima
3. Igloo
4. North Korea
5. Curd
6. Heart
7. CLINCH

Set 23
1. Hats
2. Euphrates
3. London

4. Igneous
5. Urdu
6. Moss
7. HELIUM

Set 24
1. Radium
2. European Union
3. Serious
4. Inder Kumar Gujral
5. Dasharatha
6. El
7. RESIDE

Set 25
1. Sanskrit
2. Etah
3. Cashew nut
4. Tower clock
5. Ostrich
6. Red rose
7. SECTOR

Set 26
1. Dawn
2. Uruguay
3. Serious
4. Trees
5. Europe
6. Razor
7. DUSTER

Set 27

1. Doctor
2. Yoghurt
3. Newt
4. Agree
5. Muscles
6. Odyssey
7. DYNAMO

Set 28

1. Commonwealth
2. Udaipur
3. Concave
4. Kareena Kapoor
5. Oar
6. Orange
7. CUCKOO

Set 29

1. Agree
2. Four
3. Flags
4. Ecuador
5. Cloth
6. Gandhi topi
7. AFFECT

Set 30

1. Rookie
2. Eritrea
3. Tuatara

4. Identical twins
5. Nova
6. April Fool
7. RETINA

Set 31
1. Agree
2. V.S. Naipaul
3. Sydney
4. Wales
5. Eyewitness
6. Rajendra Prasad
7. ANSWER

Set 32
1. Agree
2. Fennel
3. Republic Day
4. Ice
5. Compass
6. Abracadabra
7. AFRICA

Set 33
1. Indigo
2. New Zealand
3. Joking
4. Uttar Pradesh
5. Rajdhani Express
6. Earthworm
7. INJURE

Set 34
1. Serious
2. Web
3. Indonesia
4. Turmeric
5. C. Rajagopalachari
6. Helium
7. SWITCH

Set 35
1. Under
2. Red blood cells
3. Agree
4. Nelson Mandela
5. Ukraine
6. Seven
7. URANUS

Set 36
1. Malta
2. Oranges
3. Newton
4. David Dhawan
5. A.P.J. Abdul Kalam
6. Yolk
7. MONDAY

Set 37
1. Fingernails
2. Roger
3. Europe

4. The Netherlands
5. Cameras
6. Humayun
7. FRENCH

Set 38
1. Lemuel
2. Agree
3. Wombat
4. Yeti
5. Eden Gardens
6. Rajasthan
7. LAWYER

Set 39
1. *Baghban*
2. 1 Euro
3. Harsha Bhogle
4. Arunachal Pradesh
5. Lhasa Apso
6. Five
7. BEHALF

Set 40
1. Tamarind
2. Irfan Pathan
3. *Maqbool*
4. Bihar
5. Earth
6. Russia
7. TIMBER

Set 41
1. Daffodil
2. India
3. The Mahabharata
4. Paris
5. Lever
6. Eye
7. DIMPLE

Set 42
1. Monkey
2. Agree
3. Rani Mukherjee
4. Brahmaputra
5. Lakshmana
6. Eiffel Tower
7. MARBLE

Set 43
1. Mali
2. Agree
3. Twist
4. Tata
5. Eagle
6. Rana
7. MATTER

Set 44
1. Parashurama
2. Australia
3. Rajkumar Hirani

4. L.K. Advani; he was born in Lahore
5. Dalai Lama
6. East
7. PARADE

Set 45
1. Crescent moon
2. Agree
3. Nasik
4. Dog Star
5. Legend
6. East Germany
7. CANDLE

Set 46
1. Greenhouse gases
2. The Oscars
3. Lake
4. Din-i-Ilahi
5. Esha Deol
6. New Zealand
7. GOLDEN

Set 47
1. Painter
2. Elevator
3. Rasmalai
4. Index
5. Subhas Chandra Bose
6. Himachal Pradesh
7. PERISH

Set 48
1. Samudragupta
2. Itanagar
3. Mango
4. Pakistan
5. Lotus
6. Euro
7. SIMPLE

Set 49
1. Star
2. Cobra
3. Right-handed
4. Agree
5. Punjab
6. Earthenware
7. SCRAPE

Set 50
1. Michael Schumacher
2. Agree
3. Swimming
4. Sunderbans
5. Indira Gandhi
6. Fluorine
7. MASSIF